Exploration in Awareness
Finding God by Meditating
with Entheogens

by John E. Aiken

RONIN
Berkeley, CA

Exploration in Awareness
Finding God by Meditating
with Entheogens

by John E. Aiken

Explorations in Awareness

Copyright 2016 by Ronin Publishing
ISBN: 978-1-57951-232-3

RONIN Publishing, Inc.
PO Box 3436
Oakland CA 94609
www.roninpub.com

Production:
    Derivative author: Beverly A. Potter, PhD
    Editor: Mike Marinacci
    Book Design: Beverly A. Potter, PhD
    Cover Design: Beverly A. Potter, PhD

Distributed to the trade by **Publishers Group West**

Library of Congress Card Number: 2016941115

This is a derivative of John Aiken's 1966 self-published 85-page book created by Beverly Potter. *Explorations in Awareness*, plus additional material from *Fate Magazine* and *Journal of Borderland Research*, along with material created by Docpotter.

Acknowledgement

Thanks to *Fate Magazine* and *Journal of Borderland Research* for generously providing permission to reprint John Aiken's writings. Thanks to Mike Marinacci for finding this gem.

Table of Contents

INTRODUCTION

One of the least-studied aspects of the Sixties Psychedelic movement is the emergence of the "Psychedelic Churches". These are organized groups that sought to communalize the hallucinogenic experience, and to obtain the same legal protection—or at least cultural recognizance—for their practices that the historic substance-using religions and sects had been afforded theirs. Classified by American religious historian J. Gordon Melton as "Drug-Related Groups" in his "Western Esoteric" taxonomic family of faiths, these small but influential sects and informal circles expanded the post-modern Western understanding of the spiritual and meditative experience, and helped define the outer limits of U.S. First Amendment freedoms for self-described religious organizations.

Altered States

Humanity, according to authorities ranging from historians to pharmacologists to theologians, has almost universally pursued altered consciousness through the use of intoxicants. Quite a few ancient and historical cultures have blessed various psychotropic substances as sacraments, and gates to the Divine when used in sacred or ceremonial contexts. The mysterious *Soma* substance was the holy host of the ancient Aryans, and the Scythian warriors mourned their dead with clouds of cannabis smoke. In the far North, Siberian shamans sought visions with the powerful *Amanita muscaria* mushroom, while in the New World, Mayans ate psilocybin fungi to commune with God. The legendary Hassan I Sabbah's Ismaili jihadists were given tastes of the Hereafter's pleasures when their master fed them hashish and opium, and even the ancient Greeks may have used ergot—the organic precursor of LSD—to program Eleusinian-Mysteries celebrants for ecstasy and life-changing experiences. Catholic and Jewish sacramental wine remain in our times as reminders of how our distant ancestors sought chemical-based Epiphany.

Repressed or otherwise sidelined for centuries, the practice of intoxicant-based sacramentalism reemerged in the West in the 20th Century. In Edwardian England occultist Aleister Crowley dosed attendees of his "Rites of Eleusis" mystery-plays with peyote – the psychedelic cactus that American Indians ingested to "talk with Jesus". Decades later, the 1960 case *State of Arizona vs. Mary Attakai* established the Native American Church's peyote usage as a legitimate religious practice in the USA. *LIFE* magazine published a story about the "rediscovery" of a Mexican Indian psilocybin-mushroom cult by amateur mycologist R. Gordon Wasson.

Psychedelic Seekers

During this period Drs. John and Louisa Aiken were coming to terms with the deaths of their two adult sons, respectively killed in airplane and car accidents. Drawing on the traditions of their American Indian neighbors in Socorro, New Mexico, the Aikens experimented with peyote as a path to psychological and spiritual healing, as well as a visionary quest to satisfy their deepest personal questions about the ultimate nature of life and reality. Finding a ready audience and fellowship for their quest, they retired from their respective medical practices to form The Church of the Awakening in 1963, so that non-Indian seekers on the Peyote Road might be given the same legal opportunities to obtain succor and vision from the cactus buttons that the indigenous peoples had received.

Like their contemporary High Priest of Psychedelic Communion, then-Harvard professor Timothy Leary, the Aikens were well-educated, middle-aged professionals largely uninfluenced by the pre-Hippie counterculture and its affinity for drug use as both a hip pastime, and as a glimpse of alternative realities. But unlike the soon-to-be-infamous academic, the Aikens had neither a desire for a media spotlight, nor a mission to enlighten the masses to hallucinogenic spirituality. They limited their chemical ministrations to formal applicants, and made sure that trips happened under the supervision of experienced mentors, in appropriate environments. At the end of its existence, religious scholars estimate, the Church of the Awakening had turned on perhaps 400 psychedelic seekers, many of whom had taken the Sacrament under the supervision of the Aikens themselves, who roamed Sixties America in a mobile home that doubled as a traveling peyote-temple.

In the Aikens' wake came other psychedelics-using churches. Booted out of Harvard, Timothy Leary organized his followers as the League for Spiritual Discovery

(LSD), and preached the gospel of "Turn On, Tune In, and Drop Out" from his base at Mellon scion William Hitchcock's vast estate in Millbrook, New York. Also emerging from the lysergic Millbrook milieu was former school-psychologist Art Kleps' Neo-American Church, whose doctrine of "solipsistic nihilism" and comic, absurdist posturing anticipated the antics of later sects of parody and play like the Discordians, the SubGenius Foundation, and the Church of the Flying Spaghetti Monster. Down the river in Manhattan, gay activist and independent-Catholic Bishop Michael Itkin's Psychedelic Peace Fellowship made itself "open to all persons seriously interested in the relation of the psychedelic experience to the nonviolent revolutionary movement, whether or not they have used the psychedelic sacraments."

Three thousand miles away, psychedelic sects fruited from West Coast ground like psilocybe mushrooms after a rainy night. In the city considered Ground Zero of the Hippie explosion, San Francisco's John Mann formed the Church of the Tree of Life, seeking to establish still-legal psychedelic substances like San Pedro cactus as sacraments deserving of the same protected status that peyote had within the Native American Church. Across the

Timothy Leary (right) at Millbrook.

Bay in Berkeley, Sexual Freedom League founder Jefferson Poland's Psychedelic Venus Church promoted a sensual spirituality achieved through the combination of a cannabis Eucharist with group nudity and pansexual Goddess-worship.

Downstate in Laguna Beach, the Brotherhood of Eternal Love brought together bikers, surfers, and hippies in lysergic communions where subcultural social boundaries melted under the warmth of "Orange Sunshine"—the first brand-name LSD. And in the Central Valley, renegade Baptist pastor Kirby Hensley's Modesto-based Universal Life Church chartered psychedelics-using spiritual groups under its corporate umbrella, as a commitment to both his vision of total sectarian diversity, and to the American First Amendment guarantee of religious freedom.

Teachings and Practices

The psychedelic sects' teachings and practices generally reflected the metaphysical interests and pursuits of their founders and leaders. The Aikens recommended spiritual classics from sources as diverse as Krishnamurti, Evelyn Underhill, and Manly P. Hall to help Church members make sense of their entheogen experiences. Timothy Leary proffered the *Tibetan Book of the Dead* and the *Tao Teh Ching* as ideal guides for trippers, and turned modern translations of these ancient Eastern holy books into Sixties bestsellers. John Mann adapted Huichol Indian ceremonies to guide Tree of Lifers through their lysergic journeys on morning-glory seeds or Hawaiian baby-woodrose nuts. Neo-American "Chief Boo-Hoo" Art Kleps drew on the epistemologies of philosophers like David Hume and Nagarjuna to bolster his vision of reality itself as a solipsistic dream state, where such seemingly random signals as road signs and television commercials were pregnant with deep synchronistic meaning.

Yet, most of the chemical churches' core doctrinal statements were essentially libertarian and non-dogmatic, reflecting the subjectivity and ineffability of the psychedelic experience. Generally they adhered to live-and-let-live ethics, and affirmed the right of the individual to explore his/her own consciousness without government or societal interference. The sects existed for members to practice and protect these rights, and to create psychedelic communities as an alternative to both mainstream religions, and to what most saw as a repressive and materialistic American society.

Art Kleps expressed a countercultural defiance common to the hallucinogenic religionists in the Neo-American Church's irreverent *Boo Hoo Bible*:

> *Don't bother trying to curry favor with the establishment; it's a losing game. We aren't American Indians who can be patronized and isolated, congratulated on our sobriety, and all that. We have the right to practice our religion, even if we are a bunch of filthy, drunken bums.... We do not stand before the government as children before a parent, the government stands before us as the corruptor of our God-given human rights, and until the government gets its bloody, reeking paws off our sacred psychedelics and ceases to harass and persecute our members, until, indeed, every poor wretch now suffering in prison because he preferred the mystic uplift of pot to the slobbering alcoholism of the politicians is set free, our attitude must be one of uncompromising hostility.*

Denied First Amendment Protection

Both the courts and public opinion responded in kind. High-profile drug busts at the Millbrook retreat, and the eventual imprisonment of Leary over simple marijuana possession, showed that the legal and cultural Establishment wasn't buying First Amendment defenses of hallucinogen usage. When confronted with non-Indian defendants who insisted their legally-verboten chemicals were the sacraments of their faith, jurists across the country ruled that they weren't entitled to the same protection as Native American Church faithful, and upheld often-draconian penalties for possession and use, beliefs and circumstances be damned. And the spread of LSD and other hallucinogens from circles of sincere spiritual seekers, to teenagers in search of bigger and better kicks, hadn't exactly endeared the psychedelic subculture to mainstream Americans, whose support was necessary in the cultural battle over "drug" use and abuse.

Kennedy vs. *the Bureau of Narcotics and Dangerous Drugs*, a 1972 decision that denied the Church of the Awakening the legal use of peyote in its ceremonies, seemed to finally close the door on the possibility of psychedelic sacramentalism as anything more than an obscure, criminal underground movement, as *outre* and outlaw as Appalachia's snake-handling Pentecostal cults.

By the 1980s a cautious Timothy Leary was touting space migration and life extension, rather than lysergic acid, as the true paths to expanded consciousness, mindful of his years as one of America's highest-profile prison inmates. Art Kleps' Neo-American Church had dwindled to a handful of faithful who indulged the Chief Boo-Hoo's increasingly paranoiac and anti-Semitic rhetoric. The

Brotherhood of Eternal Love had transmogrified from an idealistic psychedelic fraternity into a wealthy international drug cartel, its ministers on the run from international law enforcement. And the Aikens, never towering figures in the psychedelic world despite their pioneering work in developing its spirituality, fell into dotage and obscurity, eventually passing on with little fanfare.

Renewed Interest

Yet events in the Nineties would conspire to revive new interest in hallucinogen-expanded consciousness. The Rave culture, born in the British post-punk scene, drew on the Sixties "Acid Tests" as a model for multimedia-powered mass tripping in a Dionysian, dance-fueled setting. In Nevada, the annual Burning Man Festival reinvented hippie psychedelic "Happenings" on an epic, total-participation scale, with city-sized gatherings of chemically-enhanced revelers freaking freely in the desolate alkali desert.

Lysergic-influenced writers like Terence McKenna, Robert Anton Wilson, and Daniel Pinchbeck repurposed the Sixties psychedelic-visionary experience for the era of the Internet and alphabet-soup designer drugs. Septuagenarian Timothy Leary found a new audience with the children of his original followers, exhorting cyberpunks, neo-Pagans, and Deadheads alike to discover the secrets of their own minds and "hack reality" with the resulting revelations.

And marijuana, damned through the Eighties in a neo-Reefer Madness panic as a "gateway drug", was rediscovered as both a mild, relatively-safe euphoriant, and a tool for intelligent seekers to see through the pretensions and absurdities of "normal" consciousness.

Conventional wisdom maintains that politics is downstream from culture, and the Nineties psychedelic revival seemed to be influencing American jurisprudence—this time, to the benefit of substance-using religious groups. In 2015, Ayahuasca Healings was granted legal status to administer the potent, emetic South American hallucinogen to communicants at their Elbe, Washington retreat. In staid Indiana, the First Church of Cannabis made headlines across the American media when it successfully registered with the IRS as a tax-exempt religious organization, and held pro-marijuana services largely tolerated by the law and by its culturally-conservative neighbors.

Meanwhile, respectable medical and psychological journals touted the use of psilocybin, MDMA, and other entheogens as both therapeutic substances, and possible paths to healthier and more positive human consciousness. Physicians, therapists, and scholars across American formed think-tanks dedicated to the study of the entheogens, and advocacy organizations working to change the laws regarding their use in science and therapy. Far from being a nostalgic revival, the new wave of interest in psychedelic consciousness is an integral part of a technological, philosophical, and aesthetic revolution that ushered in the 21st Century, and showed no signs of slowing in its second decade.

Written when LSD was still legal, and when psychedelic sects like The Church of the Awakening were first coming into public view, *Explorations in Awareness* stands as an early testimony of entheogenic spirituality as experienced by an educated, mature, and sensitive author. It is also an erudite view of hallucinogens in the light of the world's religious and philosophical traditions, and how the great wisdom teachings could both enhance, and be enhanced by, psychedelic chemistry. It remains a potent vision of how the psychedelic experience can change not only individual consciousness, but cultural perceptions of the Divine, the meaning of life, and existence itself, and open the "Doors of Perception" to new possibilities for all of us. . . . . . . The trip continues.

—Mike Marinacci
Author of *Weird California*
California Jesus

PART I
EXPLORATION

12 Signs
of Spiritual Awakening

1. An increased tendency to let things happen rather than to make things happen.
2. Frequent attacks of smiling.
3. Feelings of being connected with others and nature.
4. Frequent overwhelming episodes of appreciation.
5. A tendency to think and act spontaneously rather than from fears based on past experience.
6. An unmistakable ability to enjoy each moment.
7. A loss of ability to worry.
8. A loss of interest in conflict.
9. A loss of interest in interpreting the actions of others.
10. A loss of interest in judging others.
11. A loss of interest in judging self.
12. Gaining the ability to love without expecting anything.

1
WHAT ARE WE?

Throughout the ages, the Wise Ones, the pioneers of the Spirit, have told us that it was of ultimate importance that we should know OURSELVES. Superficial people have interpreted this superficially; those with insight have understood deeply. For Self-knowledge is knowledge of The Within; it is a result of the exploration of "inner space". When we find this Deep Center, we are finding the point at which we become one with the Universe. This unknown Self, in this unexplored country, is "the germinal higher part", spoken of by William James, which he said is "coterminous and continuous with a MORE of like quality". When we find THAT, we are in contact with the ALL.

We are finding that the cove is one with the great ocean, in its qualities. And this Self, this "I", and the Father, indeed are one. This "I" is "The Way"; it is "Truth", and it is "Life". It is the resurrection, the bread of life, the new birth. The Teacher has said, 'The things that I do, you can do also, when this 'I' becomes one with the Father"— when you find that your "I" and "The Father" are one. Not that you can, or should, perform feats that seem supernatural, or miraculous; but that you can, and should become (as He did) that Christ Self which is your inherent nature. This we do as we learn to identify with, and as that Self, that Christ, which is Consciousness, which is Life Itself, rather than with the form in which that life is manifesting, or the personality which is a by-product.

As we look back over the great panorama of the history of the universe, we see the stirrings of the Godhead; we see waves, or vortices, in the sea of universal energy. These localized disturbances are initiated by Universal Power, directed by Universal Mind or Intelligence. They are mutually attracted (by Universal Love), and the galaxies are formed. Systems are organized. Planets circle their suns. Consciousness, or Life, is started upon the long search for awareness of Itself.

Within the atom we find a basic relationship between form and energy. Waves and particles seem indistinguishable; but soon there is no question that something is happening. Energy, consciousness, is taking form, as atoms combine to produce molecules—a step towards further complexity.

We focus our attention upon the planet Earth and see the dry land appear, the seas receding. Life is taking form, and manifests as mineral, where intelligence produces in each its characteristic patterns—often beautiful crystals. Evolution is on its way, and soon from the inorganic world we begin to see traces of the organic world. Forms appear which are, or seem to be, independent of the mass. Experimentation spreads with lavish hand many various forms which we call plants. Animals begin to roam the surface of the planet, or swim in its seas. Consciousness is evolving form, through which it may manifest, and by means of which it will some day become aware of Itself. The human form arrives, and with it, Self-consciousness— at least as a possibility.

Temple of the Holy Spirit

We have not yet become accustomed to our new home, this human form, which is the temple of the Holy Spirit of Consciousness, of Life. For so many years, so many of us still identify ourselves as the form, rather than as the Spirit, the Self, which is the inhabitant of that form. Our feet are still caught in the clay of our origin. But as we look back, we become aware of the upward spiral of Life: from the basic, undifferentiated state, in which it appears as the energy within the atom—to the intelligence which manifests a crystal—to life reaching toward the sun in the forms of the plants—to the animal world as simple consciousness—to man, with a new potential, Self-consciousness. Or perhaps we may see it as a convergence, from the seething, undifferentiated energy of Space, coalescing to form that which appears to us as matter, and further focusing as smaller units of Life until We come to the Deep

Center which we, as Self-conscious units, find within ourselves—this Center of Awareness.

When we find this Deep Center, which is "The Kingdom of Heaven within", we are becoming awake to the
meaning of life. We are becoming Life Itsel—aware of Itself.
Then we are finding ourselves as Eternity in time, as Infinity
in Space. Life (or Consciousness, or God) IS, without past,

It is time to present or future; without beginning
AWAKEN. or end. "Before Abraham was, I AM!"

To find this Self, we must, at least for
a time, shift our focus from the form; we must realize our
true nature as Life, which for the time being is using a given
form. The form is constantly changing, but Life always
IS. It has been said that science is the study of the laws of
change, but science is constantly searching for the unchang-
ing Reality which is beyond change. Religion also is a search
for that Reality which changes not, and which "neither
slumbers nor sleeps".

At some time or other, each of us begins to take fal-
tering steps on the Path which will, some day, lead us to
Self-realization, towards identifying as Life, rather than as
the form in which it appears; towards identifying as Spirit, rather than as the body of matter which has clothed
it for its appearance in a material world. For many, these
first steps may come as a result of some type of what is
now called "extra-sensory perception", or ESP. We have
a dream, which we later experience as a waking reality,
and we call it "precognition". We know, before someone
speaks, what he is going to say, and we call it "telepathy".
A life which has passed beyond the physical level speaks to
us, and we call it "spirit communication". We see the power of mind over matter, as in laboratory experiments (or
other!) with dice, and we call it "psycho-kinesis" or P-K.

Such experiences are voices calling to us to recognize the fact that we are more than we have thought we were. We are more than these bodies, with which we have for so long identified ourselves! We are more even than the minds, with which some of us had begun to identify ourselves! We are LIFE, which is the Reality manifesting in bodily form, and of which even the mind is only a tool.

From *Journal of Borderland Research* Vol.19, No. 6 ,
September 1963, by permission

2

WE ARE MORE

For long, man has sought to know himself, and many have considered this to be the highest achievement. The philosophers and the laymen have sought. There have been many verbalizations but only occasional insight. The great Teachers have known their true Identity and have longed to share the experience with others, who would not, or perhaps could not, accept it. Jesus, in his longing to share this wondrous secret, cried out, "O! Jerusalem! How often would I have gathered you as a hen gathers her chicks, -- but you would not!"

Even the Masters, however, have been able only to point the way to Self-knowledge, and most of their disciples, instead of following the pointing, have deified the pointers! The Masters have told us that the Way was narrow, perhaps, as a razor's edge, and found by way of a "little gate, which most men miss because they are looking for a larger and more impressive entrance." Few have found the Way, but those few have changed the face of our world, by changing the heart of the world.

We are more than we thought we were.

The gate is said to be straight and narrow, the rigors of the Path most demanding -- but the rewards are very great. Few, however, can forego an immediate pleasure for a delayed happiness which is bliss incomparable; for this requires both faith and effort, apparently rare commodities in our world. Then, too, it is difficult to believe that the rewards are as great as the mystics tell us they are. To achieve the wisdom of a Buddha, or the love of a Christ, seems beyond our capacities. We just cannot believe that Jesus meant what he said when he told us that "Greater things than these shall you do!" Oh, we of little faith!

Only a generation or so ago, our understanding was that matter and energy were somehow separate and irreducible to anything else, or to each other; while mind was yet something else again! But  today, the lines are becoming more and more blurred. Scientists are not so sure that matter and energy are basically different the one from the other, and mind is beginning to be seen as a property inherent in matter itsel—or perhaps matter is coming to be seen as a property of mind! We are coming closer and closer to a unitary philosophy, where matter, energy and mind are perhaps different ways in which we perceive, or conceive of, the one basic underlying Reality.

This underlying Reality is beyond the reach of both body and mind, and must be realized or experienced by a still higher faculty, which we may call Intuition, Unitary Consciousness, or Cosmic Consciousness. No one can define Life, or Consciousness, or God—for to define is to limit, and Life, or God, is not subject to limitations. IT is omniscient, omnipotent, omnipresent Reality, which we can experience, because THAT is basically what we ARE. To realize this is to become AWAKE. Too long we have slept, dreaming that we are these bodies, or these minds. It is time to AWAKEN, to know our selves, to begin to live as children of our Father.

Explore Inner Space

This, then, is the challenge of the Undiscovered Country, the call to explore Inner Space. This is what is symbolized in the search for the Holy Grail, and in the attempts of the alchemist to transmute a base metal into gold. We ARE the universe of Life, and of Love, and not lumps of clay, moving feebly in a cold and lifeless environment!

This exploration, however, is not child's play. It is not a matter of reading a book (so many are seeking for the "right" one, which will give the "right" answers!), or of having some Teacher give us the word of truth. We would like so much to have someone do it for us; we crave a saviour who will make it unnecessary for us to work out our own salvation! But it is work, for men and women of faith, of hope, and of love. It involves laying down our little lives, that we may find LIFE. We must die to self, that we

Are we really these physical bodies, or are we, in our real nature, the Life which is temporarily incarnated in these bodies?

may live as the Christ, the Self. It is a matter of awakening to the fact that to realize this Self, this "treasure buried in the field" of the human ego, one must seek first this Kingdom of Heaven; he must "go and sell all that he has", to obtain this one Pearl of great price.

There are techniques and disciplines which have been pointed out by the Wise Ones and proved in practice by many to be the Way of Truth. If we are responding to this call, if we are willing to awaken from our dreams, we will invest our time and our energy. We will be patient and persistent. We will work at our Self-realizatio—though we can realize it in an instant, once we have removed the obstructions, and dropped the superfluities to which we cling so tenaciously!

When we truly and sincerely ASK, we shall be shown the Way; when we SEEK it, we shall find It; and when we KNOCK, the door to the Inner Self will be opened. This is the Law of the Way!

3

ESP CLUES

The attitudes of our culture have developed in most of us the belief that we are our physical bodies. Our mental powers are assumed to depend entirely upon the physical organism, and thought is held by many to be simply a product of the physical brain, as adrenalin is a secretion of the adrenal glands. The older orthodox religious teaching, by its emphasis on the resurrection of the physical body, in a very material heaven, only served to emphasize this type of thinking.

Today there is a surge of interest at the grass-roots level in going deeper into the meaning of life, and in seriously examining this materialistic concept to see whether it actually makes sense. There are many groups, both large and small, operating under many names and under none, who are asking such questions as "Who am I? What is the essential nature of our Being?"

The human mind can operate in areas beyond the usual physical levels.

Are we really these physical bodies, or are we, in our real nature, the Life which is temporarily incarnated in these bodies? Are we basically even these personalities with which we seem so inextricably woven? Am I really "John Doe", or "Jane Doe"? Or are we THAT which lives eternally, and which is only temporarily exploring one aspect of the Father's world, one mansion within the Father's house, as that personality? It is interesting to remember that the word "personality" originally implied a mask or a disguise! Can it be that The I, the essential Self, is only as it were playing a part for a brief time upon the stage of this earth?

Concurrent with the increasing interest in probing our essential nature has been the development of an interest in what is variously called "extra-sensory perception" (ESP), "parapsychology", or "metaphysics". All of these terms indicate an attempt to go beyond the world of materialism, whether in physics, psychology, philosophy or religion.

It seems to be the nature of what is usually called religion to become authoritarian. Religion in the time of Jesus was bound by a multitude of laws which, while meaningful at one time, had become ends rather than means. Religion consisted then in observing all of this multitude of laws, while the spiritual essence was lost. Jesus tried to awaken the church of his day to the fact that,

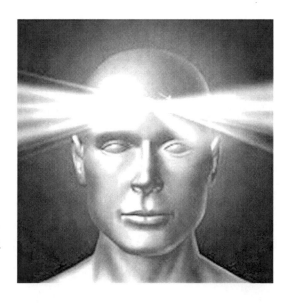

unless these laws helped men to find God, or to develop a oneness with the Father, they were of little value. You well know the reception the church gave to him!

To many people today, religion seems to have become simply organized theology, a set of beliefs or laws which we are enjoined to accept. We are then fearful of going outside this framework in order to examine whether either the beliefs or the laws are really helping us to find the Father, or whether they are becoming ends in themselves.

Research

During the past thirty years a great deal of research has been done in colleges and universities in this field of ESP, not only in this country, but throughout the world. Dr. J. B. Rhine is given credit for doing much of the earlier work in this field, demonstrating in the laboratory that the human mind can operate in areas beyond the usual physical

The phenomena of ESP are an indicaiton that there is a level of awareness beyond the physical.

levels. His findings showed that there really is such a thing as telepathy, or the awareness of happenings taking place at a distance, with no physical means of communication. He also demonstrated that there really is a mental action on material objects at a distance, a phenomenon known as "psycho-kinesis" (P-K). For example, when the mind wills that dice shall fall in a certain way, there is an effect on the way the dice do fall, even if they are not loaded!

Such laboratory demonstrations have been important in opening people's minds to a freer examination of the facts, and to the value of a little experimentation of their own.

They have encouraged many to be less fearful of the spontaneous experiences of ESP which may have happened to them. A friend, who is an anthropologist and a student of the American Indian, related with much amazement that one day when he suddenly decided to attend an Indian ceremony, he was greeted by the Indians with the statement, "You are late. We have been expecting you! "How," he asked, "did these Indians know I was going to be there when I did not even know it myself?" But he said that there were few people to whom he could even mention this experience, for they would not accept it as a reasonable possibility and would think him a very peculiar person for thinking it could be so. But many are becoming interested and are willing to look and to ask.

Interest in ESP is becoming more respectable in many scientific quarters also. The head of research at one State university, an engineer by training, is devoting part of his research program to investigating the abilities of psychics, sensitives, or mediums. He is attempting to evaluate, and to try to understand more of our mental powers which seem to operate independently of the brain and the physical body. A director of research in the Space Agency has mentioned the possibility of communication between the earth and a space vehicle by means of thought!

But where does all of this lead us? What is the meaning of it all?

The reality of telepathic communication between persons inhabiting physical bodies has been demonstrated over and over again. The evidence may be read by anyone who is interested and may be either accepted or rejected by each one, as he feels inclined. To many of us, the reality of telepathic communication between a mind inhabiting a physical body and one which is no longer in a physical body has also been demonstrated. This, of course, is more difficult for the average person to accept without personal investigation. Many of us are inclined to believe that "when we die, we are dead", and that the soul of the dead flies to some far-off Heaven where it is forever inaccessible to any form of contact with the living. Again, the evidence for the truth of the reality of communication between "incarnates" and "discarnates" may be read by anyone who is interested.

ESP & the Bible

Modern research and experimentation in the field of ESP have made much more credible intellectually many of the stories found in the Bible. In fact, from one perspective, the Bible might almost be called a manual of ESP! If we were to remove from it all of the material dealing with the extra-sensory, there would be little left! Jesus and his disciples, as well as many others, are reported to have produced not only spiritual wholeness, but physical healings, through the power of Love directed towards others. Many Bible characters speak of hearing "the voice of the Lord". Were they not perhaps receiving thoughts from another level of life which transcends the usual one ? Many speak of having precognitive dreams, which were a preview of later actual happenings.

The Bible might almost be called a manual of ESP!

Peter dreamed that a Roman officer would be coming to him for instruction and that he was to accept him, even though this was contrary to his up-bringing in the Jewish faith. At the same time, the Roman officer received instruction through a similar dream to go to Peter for further teaching.

When money was needed to pay a tax, Jesus was able to direct his followers to a spot where a fish would be caught, which carried a coin of sufficient value to make the payment. He was also able to send them to get a colt on which he might ride into Jerusalem, predicting the very words the owner of the colt would use. Many similar examples can be found in the modern literature of ESP.

The disciples who were with Jesus on the Mount of Transfiguration saw the forms of Moses and Elijah. Dr. Marcus Bach, in his book, The WIll To Believe, describes the appearance to him of the form of a sister who had died many years before and reports his conversation with her.

In the Book of Kings we find a description of the ESP powers of the prophet Elisha, who was reporting to the King of Israel all of the plans of their enemies, the Aramites. (And modern military men have tried to use psychics in the same way!) When the King of Aram sent a large military force to capture the lone prophet, Elisha's young servant was dismayed, until Elisha prayed that the young man's eyes might be "opened". Then he saw that "they who are with us are more than they who are against us !" They were literally "surrounded by a cloud of witnesses".

Have the laws of the universe changed from that time to this ? Are not similar things being demonstrated as being true today? Certainly, many people do have "hunches", perhaps warning them not to go on a certain train or plane that later is involved in an accident. Certainly, too, many people have precognitive dreams. And a well-known psychic (the term "biological radio" is preferred in scientific circles!) reported recently that he had been invited to participate in some research at the government level. Interest in ESP, anciently taken for granted, is reviving today as our attachment to a materialistic view of life is loosening a little; and recent explorations of the field in Russia is making it more accept able to our own scientific community.

For a very large number of people, ESP is a fact of nature. This is a mental power, providing evidence that we are not limited in our perceptions to our physical senses and that the mind can operate independently of the physical brain. Fortunately, a few of our modern researchers are now less interested in accumulating more and more evidence that ESP happens than they are in trying to find out how it happens—discovering more of the laws of the mind.

Life is a Process

Life is a process. It is continuous growth, continuous expansion of awareness—in other words, "evolution". The higher seems always to have its origin in the lower. Out of instinct develops intellect and reason; from simple consciousness of the animal comes the self-consciousness of the human level. And so, from self-consciousness should come that which surpasses it, which we may call "Cosmic Consciousness" or "Christ Consciousness". The phenomena of ESP are an indicaiton that there is a level of awareness beyond the physical, and beyond the usually accepted limits of the mental level.

Acceptance of the phenomena of ESP opens the door to an awareness of the reality of the next level, sometimes called the "astral" of life. Perhaps the phenomena of ESP takes place in this area, and there are some who can tune in with this level, where the frequency rate is only slightly above the limits of our normal perception. The Russians are reported to be using the term "biological radio" for a person who has this capacity.

The phenomena of ESP—telepathy, clairvoyance, clairaudience, precognition, communication with discarnates, spiritual healing, and the like—are fascinating to the novice and also very useful in our daily living. But where does all of this lead us? What is the meaning of it all? Is there not something beyond both the intellectual and the astral?

May we not recognize that there is a level of consciousness which transcends the astral and which comes even closer to the Heart of Reality? Is not this level the one which Jesus indicated when he says, "Seek first the Kingdom of God, and all these things will be added to you." One of our hymns speaks of "The Place of Quietness, close to the heart of God", which has been discovered by the mystics of all times, of all religions. This Place of Quietness is to be found by each of who seeks for it, within his own "Deep Center". It is the Inner Light of the Quaker; The Christ of St. Paul (when he sayss, "It is no longer I who live, but Christ who lives through me"); The Father, of which Jesus speaks when he says, "It is not I (Jesus) who do these things, but the Father who does them". It is the Atman of the Hindu, and his Liberation; the Bodhi onlightenment of the Buddhist—and the Mystic Vision of many Christians. This is "the treasure buried in a field" of the parable—the Divinity hidden within the human form. This is the "pearl of great price", which we are fully justified in giving up all that we have, and all that we are. When we find THIS and become THIS, then truly "The I and The Father are one!"

4

PARABLE OF THE ACORNS

Thre was once a very busy Acorn community, high in an oak tree. For the most part, all were happy in fulfilling what they considered to be the ultimate purpose of life—to become better Acorns. To this end the activities of their schools were devoted. They had their service clubs—such as Acorn Rotary, whose motto was "Better Service for Better Acorns!" There were many self-help programs to promote the cause of better Acorn-ness. There were even Acorn Beauty Shops, to polish and improve the appearance of the shell! And some of the Acorns had a wonderful polish; their shells were beautiful!

Some of the Acorns were not satisfied, however, because for some reason they could not convince themselves that to have a highly polished shell, or just to help another Acorn to have a high polish, was the ultimate purpose of life. Naturally, such Acorns were resented by the majority in the community, for it is not pleasant to have one's complacency upset.

There was also one disturbing thought which could not always be supressed by any Acorn. It seemed that, at some time, each Acorn must fall to the ground. The shell, no matter how highly polished, would split, moisture would seep in, and what was called death would come to that Acorn. And so, occasionally even some of the orthodox majority among the Acorns would wonder (although feeling rather guilty for doing so!) whether the real purpose of Acorn life was only to become better and better Acorns.

What Happens at Death

The Acorn Priests, however, were reassuring. It had been revealed to them, so they said, that at the time of death (provided, of course, that during his life he had obeyed all of the priestly commands) each Acorn would immediately be transported to Acorn Heaven where Acorns did not fall, nor leaves lose their green-ness; where it would be possible for them to sit at the right hand of the Acorn God; and where they would be Acorns Immortal, forever. There was even a ritual which the priests would perform (for a fee, of course) over the spot where the Acorn had fallen to the ground.

The Prophet said that Acorns were not primarily "acorns", but that their true nature was "Oakness".

The appearance later of a plant springing up at this spot was the assurance that the Acorn had in truth passed on to Acorn Heaven, to become an Immortal Acorn.

The time came, however, when the Acorn community was aroused by the teachings of an Acorn Prophet who had the temerity to say that the Acorn People were being

misled by the Priests. "Although it is important to be a good Acorn," he said, "the ultimate purpose of life is not merely to become better and better Acorns, to develop a more and more highly polished shell." He taught that the ultimate purpose of life was "unfoldment", or "finding the Kingdom of Heaven which is within each Acorn". He said that Acorns were not primarily "acorns", but that their true nature was "Oakness"; and that genuine fulfillment in life came only when an Acorn could "realize", or make real, this inherent Oak-nature. Even the falling to the ground, he said, was only a step in this process of Self-ealization, of becoming THAT which each one truly was, and that the ceremonies of the priests had no effect on the ultimate destiny of the "Acorn-becoming-Oak".

The angry Acorn Priests called on the Acorn Scientists, to see if they could not refute such teachings. The Acorn Scientists carefully examined a number of Acorns, after which they prepared scholarly papers which pointed out how illogical it was to believe in the existence of such "Oakness"—which could not be seen, heard, touched, tasted or smelled! "Even with our ultra-microscopes, we find no evidence of this Oakness which this deluded Prophet has declared to be the essential nature of all Acorns," they wrote. The Acorn people heard the report and bowed reverently to this wisdom—for did not the Scientists know all things ?

But the Acorn Prophet radiated such Love and Wisdom that for a time he acquired a large following, which further angered the Priests and the merchants. "The whole community is going mad, and following after this uncouth fellow," they said. "Something must be done about it, or he will ruin our business!" And so the Priests turned him over to the courts and had him crucified—thinking thereby to put an end to his nonsense. Such was not entirely the case, however, for a few remembered his love and his wisdom, and tried to follow his teachings, tried to unfold that Oakness which was their real Self, their basic Nature.

Those who really followed the teachings of the Acorn Prophet, who attempted to realize their Oakness, became so tranquil and so glowing (and the glow seemed to come from within, not from a mere surface polish) that again the multitudes were attracted. And so, in order to save their position, the Acorn politicians and the priestly hierarchy took over the teachings, which they carefully reworded to make them harmless—and claimed that they had been the authors of them .all the time!

And so it came about that the teachings of the Acorn Prophet were no longer followed, but that he was worshiped as the one and only Incarnation of Oakness. It was taught that the way to become an immortal Acorn was to believe this, and to follow the rituals set up by the Acorn Priests! It became blasphemous to say that each Acorn was potentially Oak, and heresy not to believe that the Acorn Prophet was the one and only Incarnation of Oakness!

A few, however, remembered the teachings of the Prophet, when he said that the basic nature of each Acorn was Oak, and in realizing this Oak Self, they developed a tranquillity and a peace which could not be understood.

5

WHO AM I?

Most of us consider the physical body, or perhaps the personality, in which we will include the body-mind-emotions complex, as the Self. But, in our search for understanding, we come to the realization that the Self is much more than the body or personality.

A better understanding of the Self may be gained through the analogy of the amoeba, a single-celled organism. It looks like a microscopic drop of egg-white, and has a flowing sort of motion. It can capture a food particle by extending a part or projection of itself to enfold the particle. This projection or "pseudopod", with the food, is then retracted into the larger body.

The main body of the amoeba may represent the I AM, the Individuality. This Individuality, the larger Self, desiring the experience of an earth" life, then projects a "pseudopod", which appears on the earth plane as an ego, a personality, which is given a name as "John Doe"—indicated by "JD".

John Doe, then, is simply a projection or manifestation of the I AM, the larger Self; John Doe is an experience which "I" am having. The "I" is experiencing an earth life, via its projection, the personality, John Doe. When Jesus said, "I AM the Way", was

I AM, and John Doe is simply an experience which is happening to ME.

he not referring to this I AM, which is the higher Self of each one of us,—The Christ, with which Jesus identified himself completely? Figure 1 indicates that the I AM itself is a "projection" of the Universal, which is God, or "The Father". Therefore, we may say that "I AM an experience which the Father is having"! "The Father", through the I AM, is manifesting as John Doe; John Doe is therefore an incarnation—an appearance in the flesh—of the Father.

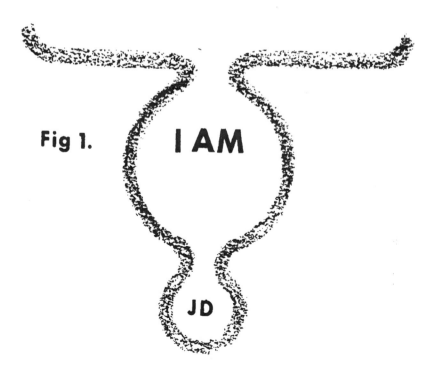

Fig 1.

I AM

JD

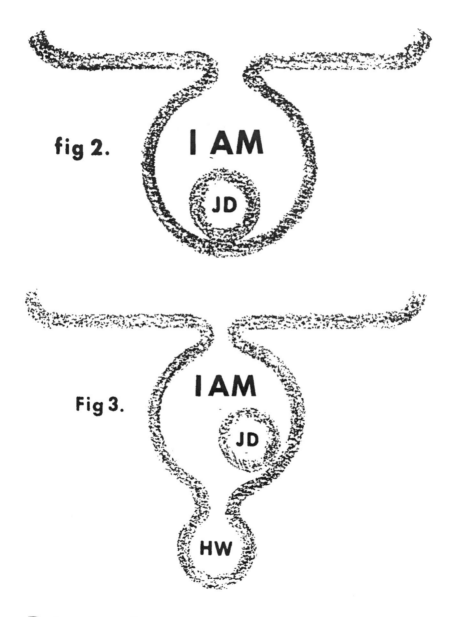

fig 2.   I AM   JD

Fig 3.   I AM   JD   HW

Reincarnation

The same analogy may also be useful in arriving at an understanding of reincarnation, and of what it is that reincarnates. Figure 1 indicates that "I" am experiencing life as John Doe. Figure 2 indicates that John Doe has died—that the physical manifestation, the pseudopod, has disappeared from the earth level—but that "I" continue to exist. "I" have always existed. "Before Abraham was, I AM!" And I have been nourished and enriched by the experiences which "I"have had as John Doe.

John Doe will never exist again, but "I" always AM. I may wish further earth experiences, and so I project another personality, which is named "Henry Williams" (HW), whose subconscious or larger Self is modified by MY previous experiences as John Doe. In turn, Henry Williams disappears from the earth level, and I have been enriched by his earth life also. This appearance and disappearance, at the earth level, of personalities may continue as long as I feel the need or desire for earth experiences.

Let us now suppose that Henry Williams during his earth lifetime is placed in a hypnotic trance, and regression to a previous lifetime suggested. Hypnosis seems to have the effect of breaking through the barrier, indicated by the constriction between the I AM and the personality. And so, under hypnosis, Henry speaks of having once been John Doe, because he then has access to the total consciousness of the I AM which contains these memories.

With the help of Figure 4, we can visualize a relationship which indicates that I and my brother I are also one, in "The Father". Henry Williams and Hazel Smith, apparently separate projections or incarnations on the earth level, are seen both to be one with The Father and also with each other! Is not each one an expression, a manifestation, an incarnation, of God on earth? Actually, we are no more separate than are the fingers of the hand which, if

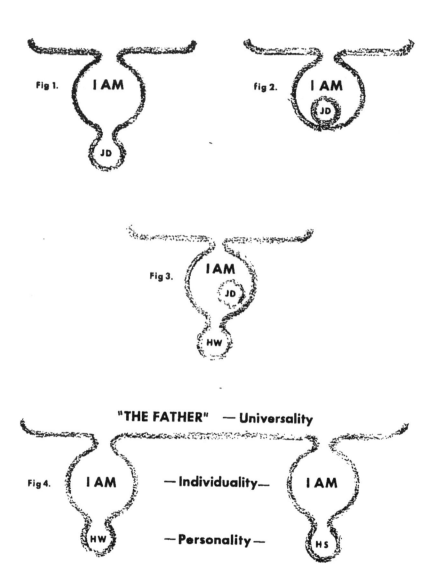

Fig 1. I AM JD

fig 2. I AM JD

Fig 3. I AM JD HW

"THE FATHER" — Universality

Fig 4. I AM — Individuality— I AM

HW — Personality — HS

really separated, as in an accident, are completely useless. "Apart from ME you can do nothing!"

The lessons of life, then, involve a series of identifications. At first, we identify with the personality: "I am John Doe." Later, we find that I AM more than John Doe. I

AM, and John Doe is simply an experience which is happening to ME. Then, still further along the way, we realize that "The Father and I are One", as indicated in all of the Figures, by the upward extensions of the I AM—and that even the personality, John Doe, and the Father are One!

Truly, there is only ONE!

6

GUILTY OR NOT GUILTY?

To achieve wholeness, integration, at-one-ment, of our entire being, the awareness of our oneness with God, with the Universe, and with our fellow man, is a basic necessity for all of us. But the feeling of guilt, often deep-seated and unrecognized as such, is one of the major obstacles to such achievement.

Subjectively, guilt is a feeling, or a belief, that we have wronged another, or ourselves, in some way; that we have thought, said or done something of which we, or another whose good-will we wish to have, would not approve. It is a negative, contractive, anti-life emotion that produces toxic reactions in the body, distorts our thinking, and impedes our growth or evolution. It is a prime cause of self-condemnation, self-rejection and unhappiness, and greatly reduces our ability to serve our fellows and to contribute to the growth of our society.

Sources of Guilt

Guilt feelings arise, first, from the fact that many of us have been conditioned by early training to believe that our basic nature is evil, that we are conceived and born in sin. Thus we begin life with a great emotional handicap; and because we cannot accept ourselves, cannot love our- *No one can step into the same stream twice.* selves, we cannot love any other, in the highest sense of the word. Even when we learn intellectually, later in life, that there is no logical reason for such a belief, we have not thereby eliminated this factor at the subconscious level where it continues to affect, as a general undertone, all of our attitudes toward life.

Guilt also arises as a result of traumatic emotional experiences, especially during childhood, which further impress us with our own unworthiness, and contribute to our self-rejection.

Dorothy, aged five, was overheard by her mother calling her younger brother a fool. She was promptly spanked, and at the same time told of the Biblical warning that he who calls his brother a fool is in danger of hell fire". Dorothy was thereby convinced that she was a lost soul, and in the next 40 years was in and out of mental hospitals several times for the treatment of a depressive psychosis.

When Dorothy matured, she became a student of philosophy and religion, and knew intellectually that there was no basis for the belief that she was irrevocably "lost" because of her display of temper in childhood. But this did not change in the least the conviction, at the sub-conscious, action level, that her situation was hopeless. She was released from this guilt only by a day of intensive therapy when under the effects of a psychedelic chemical. She is now able truly to love God and her neighbor, because she can truly accept herself.

Another major source of guilt is our awareness of the obvious gap between our actions and our knowledge. We all know so much better than we do; we all do so much less than we know! Why, then, is this so? Is it not because our actions are governed only in part by our knowledge? Are they not also affected, and perhaps even to a much greater extent, by our emotions, by our old habit patterns, and by the pressure of circumstances at the moment of action? Are they not the result of our heredity, our environment, the current mores, and our previous emotional and intellectual conditioning, as well as of our knowledge of what is right action in any given circumstance ?

To better understand our situation, we might suggest the analogy of the wagon train, breaking a new trail through rough, mountainous country. An advance party of scouts is sent ahead to find the best route for the wagon to follow, through the new and difficult terrain. In this analogy, the scouts represent our knowledge, the intellect;

Each step is most important at the time we are ready to take that step!

the wagons represent the will, which produces our actions, our conduct. In every case the knowledge of the scouting party is far ahead of the actions of the wagon train in applying this knowledge. By force of will, by effort and hard work, the wagon train is brought to the place where the scouts said it should be. But in the meantime, the scouts have gone far ahead, finding the way to be followed. And so there is always a gap between the knowledge of the scouting party (the intellect) and the application of this knowledge by the wagons (the will, expressed in action). It seems that there is always—and should be!—a gap between our knowing and our doing, between intellect and will. If this were not so, there would be no progress, no growth!

Is there any reason for the wagon-drivers to feel guilty because their wagons do not always keep up with the scouting party? Many obstacles, many boulders in the path, have to be surmounted or removed for the passage of the wagons, which were no hindrance to the scouts. Should there be condemnation, so long as effort is being applied to this end ? Let us be grateful to the intellect for performing its function as a path-finder; and to the will for its more difficult function as a path-follower!

There is no condemnation of the infant who is learning to walk because he falls many times in his learning; and we see no evidence of guilt on his part because of his falls. Do we not encourage him to get up and try again ? Perhaps we might even say that failure is the road to success, for by failing we learn how not to fail.

Still another source of guilt feelings may be observed in our tendency to condemn ourselves as we look back on our actions of some past time. It is quite obvious that we should have acted with a great deal more wisdom! The infant really should not have fallen down in his learning to walk! And so we condemn ourselves for our past failures, and develop a great feeling of guilt for this reason.

Failing Teaches Wisdom

However, we fail to note that, in so doing, we are judging and condemning "another"—a person who no longer exists! Today, as we look back on past actions, we no longer are that person who sinned by unwise actions in some yesterday. Our past failures have taught us some degree of wisdom, in the light of which our past actions seem rather foolish; but for this very reason, we no longer are that person of the past. It is said that no one can step into the same stream twice—or speak to the same person twice, for both he and we have changed. The body itself changes completely, so that no one of us has the same physical body he had only a few years ago. The mind is constantly changing, as new experiences add to our knowledge and make some slight contribution to wisdom. And so perhaps the injunction, "Judge not, that you be not judged", applies to ourselves as well as to others!

As to judging others, let us recall the incident of the pupil who related to his teacher the story of a problem which he had faced, and his solution. He was uncertain as to whether his actions under the given circumstances would be approved by his teacher, and so he asked, "If you were I, what would you have done?" Is there not only one possible answer to this question? The teacher replied, "If I were you, I would have done exactly as you did!" You will note that the question as put was not, "If you, with your understanding, were faced with this situation, what would you do?" This would be an entirely different matter.

It would be of tremendous help to any of us if we could only remember, as we observe the actions of any person, "If I were he, I would be doing exactly as he is doin—under the pressures to which he is subjected, and with his understanding, or lack of it."

Such an insight, applied to ourselves, or to the person we consider "our-self of the past, can be a factor in relieving the feeling of guilt for past unwisdom. "Today, given the same situation, and with only the understanding I had then, and with all of the pressures, emotional as well as intellectual, and the strength of old habit patterns, I would do exactly as I did then!" Of course, this can never happen, for we no longer are the same persons. The habit patterns have changed, at least a little, and the same situation can never duplicate itself.

Some may feel that to eliminate this feeling of guilt for our past failures, or for our present inadequacies, is simply to offer an alibi for such failures, an excuse for not changing our present bad habits. But such is not the case; effort and improvement are encouraged. If we are relieved of this load of guilt, then we have so much more energy available for the task at hand.

Rather than berating himself for his failure to have the wagon at the point indicated by the scouting party, the driver will be much more effective if he puts his shoulder to the wheel!

7

THE CIRCLE OF LIFE

In evaluating the various aspects of life, one needs a frame of reference, a perspective, that will include all of them. When this is achieved, it is readily seen that no phase is less important, nor more important, than any other. Each is a step on the Way, a lesson to be learned, experience to be gained.

The story which Jesus told of the youth who insisted on having his inheritance in advance, so that he might explore the world, provides a useful structure for the understanding of life. It seems much more useful if the path of the Prodigal Son is visualized as circular, rather than straight-line—out to the far country and return. On such a circular path, each step the young man takes away from his Father's house is also a step towards his Father's house, for even when going away from home, he is nevertheless going towards home.

All things are seen to be exactly as they should be! The centrifugal force of his urge to explore the world is balanced by the centripetal force of Love, and he is inevitably brought back to his beginning—which is also going forward to his destiny.

Interest in the Physical

Let us apply this analogy of the Prodigal Son to our own journey through life. Each one of us goes through a stage in his earlier years of primary interest in the physical. The infant finds his fingers, his toes; he explores objects in his immediate environment; he experiments with his senses.

Most of us adults are but spiritual infants, whose primary interest is in the physical. We are fascinated by our toys, our gadgets - automobiles, airplanes, space vehicles

But this exploration of our physical environment is a necessary prelude to other phases of life and not at all to be condemned. For those to whom it is all-important, it is all-important! The lessons learned in the earlier grades of our school system are by no means of any less importance than those learned later, for the lessons learned in these years form the basis for all subsequent learning. And so those of our friends who are engrossed in the exploration and enjoyment of the material aspects of life are doing exactly what they should be doing—taking an important step on the way Home!

The Intellect

After the basic exploration of the physical or material aspects of life, comes the strong interest in its intellectual aspects. The possibilities of the mind become most fascinating, and a whole new world opens up to us. For a time, the intellect is all! If we can not fit Reality into our particular intellectual framework, then it must not be Reality! A psychologist recently commented that even if certain phenomena were true, he would not accept them, because this would destroy his carefully constructed pattern of reality.

We are likely, in constructing this fascinating intellectual world within our own consciousness, to assume the truth of a certain premise—such as one that would regard the physical world as all of Reality—and then to accept the truth only of those ideas which are consistent with this basic premise, which itself may not be true. We build a world of concepts, forgetting that Reality is not a concept; that any concept of Reality is not Reality! Reading about the ocean is not the ocean; concepts about it are no substitute for experiencing it. And this experience can be infinitely varied, always changing, never-ending, having little relationship to words, whether on paper or spokenor to concepts or ideas! Concepts are only shadows of Reality, and words are only shadows of concepts. And yet, there is a fascination about this attempt to conceptualize about experience, and to verbalize our concepts—as I am doing now!

However, this conceptualizing, and verbalizing of concepts, certainly is one aspect of the joy of the exploration of Life, and so is as important as any other. It is another step on this circular path which leads Home—and which also we have conceptualized and verbalized!

As we follow this "Circle of Life", the time comes inevitably when we have new interests developing. We begin to wonder whence we have come, how we happen to be here, and what the meaning of it all might be. Who or What are we?? Is there a non-material, or even a non-intellectual

Truth is not in words, but in experience, of which words can be only a pale shadow.

Reality, which somehow transcends and yet includes both the physical and the intellectual? Is there an aspect of life which might be called "spiritual", the exploration of which takes us farther on this path of the unfolding of Being ? If this is so—and certainly many have found it to be sothen this is but another step on the Homeward Journey and, if we can see it so, neither more nor less important than any other. Each step is most important at the time we are ready to take that step! Without having taken the first step, we would not be ready to take the second, or the tenth—or the last!

Spiritual Aspects

When we become ready for the exploration of the "spiritual" aspect of life, our awareness, which has been focused primarily on the physical, or the mental, now begins to turn within, seeking to know Itself. We begin to find new and deeper meaning in the writings of the mystics. A new level of awareness—which is variously called Intuition, Christ or Cosmic Consciousness, Satori, Liberation, Nirvana—begins to unfold, and our activities begin to express more of Wisdom and Love.

There is the experience of the Unity of all things, the conciliation of the opposites. There is no longer any separation between man and God but the realization that "The Father and the I are One". The positive and the negative are found to be two poles of a oneness. The scientist who had found the universe to be "less a Great Machine than a Great Thought, projected by a Great Thinker", now becomes aware that there is no separation of Thinker, Thought, and Mechanism. All are experienced as a great, all-inclusive Whole which may be expressed, depending on the cultural back-ground of the one expressing, as The Great Void, The Continuum, or The Kingdom of Heaven Within of which Jesus spoke.

In our attempt to analyze THAT which cannot be analysed, we find that besides the experience—not the concept !—of Unity which has been mentioned, there is also the experience—not the concept!—of Perfection. All things are seen to be exactly as they should be! Intellectually, of course, we know that this is not so. There should not be wars, famine, disease, death! But even intellectually we can recognize the fact that, in a growing evolving world, which ours seems to be, perfection is in growth, in the moving from the lesser—which is relative imperfection—to the greater—which is relative perfection. But in its turn, the greater will then become a lesser to another greater, and so represent imperfection or "evil". In any case, as we experience even a glimpse of this larger Awareness of the Intuitional or Christ level, we experience the Perfection even of "imperfection"!

A third realization associated with this expanded awareness is the experience of Life. Life is experienced— not intellectualized, conceptualized or verbalized—as Universal Reality, manifesting as all things, and yet transcending all things. The mineral is seen to be expressing Life, Consciousness, God, in its way, just as the plant, the

animal, the human, in theirs! All is Life or God; and God or Life is ALL.

Thus, the experience of Oneness, of Perfection, and of Life, constitute an insep-

arable trinity, to provide an ineffable Awareness of Being-
ness in which there are no opposites, no imperfections. We
are then fulfilling the prayer of Jesus when he prayed "that
they might be One as we are One" that we might achieve
this Oneness with the Father which he had achieved, and
which is more than all of the trappings of life, which is
LIFE ITSELF.

The Prodigal when he comes to himself comes to his
Father. He realizes that at no time had he ever been other
than his Father's son, no matter how seemingly separated
by time or space. And so, in one sense, he really had never
left home!

We completed the Circle of Life
and are AT HOME!

8

LOOK WITHIN

In directing our attention within, what do we find? Usually a jumble of thoughts and feelings; desires, frustrations, ambitions, fears, loves, hates, attractions, repulsions. If we can, even for a moment, command this storm, as a Teacher once did, "Peace! Be still!"- then, in the moment of calm, when all of these waves of thought and emotion have died down, we can see, find, experience, Truth. We can see, and become "The I Am", "The Self", "The Inner Light", "The Christ",—which is One with The Father.

Or, if we can experience for a moment what we find within when someone unexpectedly calls, loudly, "LISTEN!",—and we pause, alertly expectant, without thought or feeling, but just being open and perceptive, and receptive, we will find this same State of Being, which is not a "nothingness", nor a blankness, but a total Awareness, an Awakeness, which is Being Itself!

Or, if we will quietly and calmly observe within, watching the jumble of thoughts and feelings, we will find that the usual "inner storm" will slowly subside. Thoughts will become more widely spaced, do not follow each other quite so closely, until we will be able to find a "space", an interval, between the thoughts. If we will then at once dive into this space, we will find ourselves within our own Inner Being; we will have found the "Self, which is one with the Father—which, indeed, is the Father, for there is no separation. To find this is to fulfill the prayer of Jesus, "that they might be one as we are onethat we might find the same oneness with the Father that he had found. Did He not say, "What I have done, you can do also!"?

Does not life itself flow, as the music flows ?

Balance

To restore balance to our spiritual growth, and hence the real value of our service to others, we need to learn and practice this ancient Way of Self-discovery; for in coming to know the Inner Being which is the real Self of each of us, we find true love for both God and neighbor, and our ability for real service is thereby increased.

Can one whose well is dry give water to the thirsty ?

Wei Lang (China, 638-713) remarks that "What I can tell you is not Truth; but if you will turn the light of consciousness within yourself, there you will find Truth!" Truth is not in words, but in experience, of which words can be only a pale shadow.   But even a shadow can be useful, if it directs our attention to the Reality which has produced it

Rock of Being

When we build our 'house" on this Rock of Being, which is The Christ, instead of on the shifting sands of thought and emotion, we find the inner tranquillity which no storm in the external world can destroy; and we find ourselves becoming an increasingly clear channel through which Love can be expressed in Service.

A single experience of this Inner Light, or Self, can provide a stimulus to motivate us to further seeking. The path to this Center of our Being has been clearly marked by those who have gone before, but we ourselves must walk therein. In the beginning, at least, we need a daily regular time and place; perhaps a special corner, a special chair; when possible, a special room. For we are creatures of habit, and the development of helpful habits can save us time in the end. At first, as we seek this Mental Quiet, this inner peace and tranquillity, we catch only glimpses of the Inner Being; but gradually we acquire the ability to retain this awareness for a longer and longer time, until at last all of our living is irradiated by this glow from within. Then we have "removed our Light from underneath the bushel, and set it on the lamp-stand, so that it sheds light on all that is in the house" of our mind.

In the earlier stages of our following on the Spiritual Path, we are likely to become discouraged if spectacular

results are not achieved quickly. And yet we understand perfectly that time and endless effort are required if one is to achieve proficiency in any of the arts or sciences! Spiritual growth involves a lifetime of devotion and effort, and growth is usually unseen and un-noticed! On the spiritual Path, no effort made in sincerity is ever lost or wasted.

While at first we need to have a regular time and place, this inward turning for Mental Quiet can soon be practiced at any time, any place, under any circumstances. A voice student needs to have an hour daily devoted to the special practice of his exercises, but while this special time and place are necessary, he can also practice at any time, or in any place, whenever he chooses to do so. Ultimately, if he is a true musician, he no longer sings the music, but the music sings him!

When we have found, and become, this Inner Being, this Inward Light, how can we describe it? Words are such pale shadows! Perhaps it can be done only by saying what it is not! Has this Light any color ? or shape ? or size ? Is it related to time or space, to sound or silence?

Or do all of these originate from within this Inner Self? Is not this the finding of "The Christ, which is the Light of the World"[1]? - "The peace which passes understanding", the tranquillity which transcends that of the intellect ? Is not this true at-one-ment with the Father ? "You ARE the Light of the world" - and for one who IS the Light, there are no shadows!

May you then find this deep Center of Being, this Indwelling Christ, the Inward Light, the Atman, Nirvana, The Void - for which all names and descriptions are meaningless ! If you will seek, with your whole heart, you shall find!

9

LIFE IS NOW

Where can one find the Past ? Where is the fragrance of the rose I held yesterday ? Where is the sound of yesterday's concert? Where does the Future exist? Can it be found anywhere in time or space? Can I eat food tomorrow to satisfy my hunger NOW ? Is there a past, or a future, or is there only that perpetually renewed, fleeting instant which we call NOW?

I hold a rose in my hand. But is it really a rose? Would not a man speaking a different language call it by some other name ? Would this flower I am holding be that name, any more than it is "a rose"? Is it really "a flower"? Would not our friend of another culture have a different word, to replace "flower"? So is it not true that this "flower", which I call "a rose", is neither flower nor rose?

With seemingly endless variety, the unconscious mind employs visual and other symbolic representations to instruct the conscious mind in what it needs to know!

Is it not simply a part of "That Which Is"? In naming it in any way, are we not hiding from ourselves its real nature? And failing to achieve a full experience of that nature?

Naming Experience

I am listening to music. I say, "Yes, Beethoven's Pastoral Symphony !" Am I really listening as I am saying this ? Or even thinking this ? Or am I thinking about listening? Does not this "thinking about" interfere with genuine, complete absorption in the music ? And again, is it really "music" to which I am listening ? Would not one who speaks another language call it something else? As long as we are naming the experience of That which we call music, are we not losing some of the experience ? For is not the "music" flowing by in the meantime, and escaping us? There is of course a time for the naming—but is there not also a time for only experiencing ?

The Way is strait and narrow, and the finding and following thereof require both desire and effort.

Does not life itself flow, as the music flows ? Can we then catch it in a net of names? Or does at least a part of its fullness escape us as we are busily naming its surface?

Can we, even briefly, simply look at the rose—which is not "a rose"? Or just iisten to the music—which is not "music"? Or only be with Life, which is not "life"?

Be still—and KNOW!

10

THE SECRET PATH

The majority of those who are not satisfied to accept the dogmas of either organized science or organized religion are likely to begin their search with an investigation of the psychic area. Interest is likely at first to be centered in evidence of survival of death, and in communication with the departed—for this is an indication that there is a reality beyond the realm of the physical senses. Many go from this to an interest in, and experience

with, spiritual healing, and both interests lead naturally to an increased interest in prayer as communion with our Infinite Source. Gradually, as we develop, we begin to learn and to experience in some degree that which is termed "mystic"

No one can give us this Light, for it is already ours; and only we ourselves can discover it and realize its presence eternally within our own consciousness.

or "hidden". We begin to understand what Jesus meant by his two great commandments, for we actually experience these things.

The Secret Path is not really "secret"—but it certainly is not obvious! The Master said, "Strait is the gate, and narrow is the Way, and there are a few who find it." The Buddha said that it was "as narrow as a razor's edge". But, as the Master said, it can be found by anyone who seeks to find it. Why, then, are there so few ?

First, there are many who do not know of it; they are so immersed in materialism, in the pursuit of money and sense pleasures, that they have no opportunity to learn that there is anything else in life that is important. Second, many know vaguely of it but do not wish to find it, because they fear that such interests would make it necessary for them to give up eating the husks of a materialistic civilization—and believing the dogmas of a materialistic religion. Or, third, perhaps they are looking for a wider, easier way. A Chinese sage has said, "The entrance to the Path is by a little gate, and few find it because they are seeking a more elegant and impressive entrance." The Way is strait and narrow, and the finding and following thereof require both desire and effort. But they who seek will find and in finding achieve immortality, eternal life, which is NOW. When the window, the eye of the spirit, is open, the whole consciousness will be radiant with the light of the Sun.

Way of Self-Knowledge

The Mystic Way, the Secret Path, is the way of Self-Knowledge. It is the way to higher levels of consciousness, in which one identifies himself with his Higher Self. When we do this, we find that truly "the Father and the I are One", and we also become one with all the world. Then one truly loves God with his whole heart and his neighbor as himself! It is the way of Self-Realization, by which we learn Who we really are, transcending both body and mind, and finding the Reality of pure consciousness within, the "Inner Light" which is one with the Eternal Sun.

This mystical experience, the attaining of awareness of the Presence within, is perhaps the greatest goal of all life and the only goal for him who is seeking. It is the true, though often unrecognizable goal of all religions. Forms, ceremonies, creeds, scaraments, traditions and scriptures, all have value only as they help man to find a personal relationship with the Infinite, to realize his true Self. It is an unfolding of that which is within, as the seed unfolds the plant, fruit and seed that is "in-folded" within it. It is the realization of this Inner Power that lifts us to the Light— and the Inner Spark becomes a Flame.

No one can give us this Light, for it is already ours; and only we ourselves can discover it and realize its presence eternally within our own consciousness. "Behold, I stand at the door and knock. If any man will open ... " Even a Christ or a Buddha can only point the Way. But by following their pointing, we ourselves become the Way.

He experiences him-self as a far greater being than he had ever imagined

It is difficult even for one to point the Way for another; but that which discovers truth within our own hearts is the Word of God for us. We can only suggest to others that which has been an aid for us, in the hope that others may be helped thereby to find their Way

From *Journal of Borderland Research* Vol.19, No. 6 ,
September 1963, by permission

11

MIND-CHANGING CHEMICALS

Nature, however, may have some hidden persuaders which will make it possible for more of us to believe! Modern pharmacological research has produced a series of chemicals which affect the activities of the mind. The best known of these, of course, are the tranquilizers. These have improved our management of patients afflicted with fears and anxieties, and so have reduced the census figures of our mental hospitals. However, their main effect is, through chemical change, to enable a patient to live with his fears, to disregard his problems, not to solve them. None of these agents attacks the cause, but provides only temporary symptomatic relief, often at the price of serious side effects.

However, there seems to be greater promise in a newer series of compounds which includes lysergic acid diethylamide (LSD), mescaline, psilocybin, and a few others. They were first called "hallucinogens" because of their tendency to induce hallucinations in subjects. Common effects of this type include visual disturbances, with distortion in shape and proportions of objects (the parallel sides of a door frame seemed not parallel, and moving, in one of my own experiences). Beautiful geometric designs, often in brilliant colors, are frequently seen in objects which, to others, seem quite ordinary. One often has the feeling of seeing into an object, especially a flower or a picture. Two dimensional objects are often seen as in three dimensions -- and perhaps three dimensional objects may be seen in four dimensions! Many investigators have given vivid descriptions of such effects, especially Alan Watts in his book "Joyous Cosmology", and Jane Dunlap in "Exploring Inner Space".

These substances have been called "psychotomimetic" (simulating insanity), because many subjects tend to develop symptoms which are similar to those seen in schizophrenia, the most common mental ailment. The subject may lose to some degree his usual contact with reality -- "reality" being interpreted in this case as our usual material environment. Many develop a feeling of omnipotence, omniscience, and a feeling of "oneness" with everything in the universe. Life is seen from a different perspective, so that many things which seemed to be of great importance no longer seem so.

This ability to induce, through chemical means, a "model psychosis" or a laboratory case of temporary "insanity" has made these preparations of great interest to physicians and researchers dealing with the mentally ill, because of the new understanding of such illness which may be gained. In addition to this, it has been suggested that it is most helpful for the doctor to have the experience of taking one or more of these preparations, because it can greatly increase his understanding of the mentally ill.

A third effect of these new substances has been named, by
Dr. Henry Osmond, for many years director of the Saskatchewan Provincial Hospital, "psychedelic" or "mind-manifesting". In addition to producing hallucinations, and sometimes
simulating insanity, they tend to bring about a great increase

in the manifestation of
the powers-of-the mind.
At the physical level,
there is a great enhance-
ment of the acuity of
the senses, resulting in
greater awareness of
beauty in sound and
form. Music is heard
as it probably never
had been heard before.
Psychic powers may de-
velop, and one is often
very sensitive to the thoughts and feelings of others, or may be
aware of happenings at a distance. There seems frequently to
be an increased awareness of a level of understanding which is
superior to that contacted in our usual state of consciousness.
New perspectives are developed, and new insight into problems, so that the problems themselves vanish, or the solution
may become obvious. One alcoholic who participated re-
marked that he now understood his problems, and no longer
had any reason to drink. Unlike the tranquilizers, therefore,
these compounds definitely aid in the solution of the problems.

Nature's Mind-Changers

Yet all of this is not new. We can trace these substances back
through thousands of years; as they have been used by man
in their natural form, just as penicillin was originally a gift of

Nature, a product of a lowly mold, so the gift of the psychedelics came originally from our Great Mother. The ancient Egyptians had the Sacred Mushroom, eaten ceremonially by the priests to stimulate psychic ability and mystical experience. Our own American Indians have used parts of the peyotl cactus for centuries in their religious ceremonies. In addition, in Mexico, there are still a few who find a degree of "enlightenment" in the use of a species of mushroom. And LSD had its origin in ergot, a fungus which grows on rye.

Dangerous Addictive Drugs

Many other substances have been used by seekers for a short-cut to wisdom, such as opium, hashish or marihuana, and most widely used of all, alcohol! Occasionally anaesthetics, especially nitrous oxide, will produce a similar effect. But all of these are disappointing, in that the visions are usually of inferior quality or short duration, and some of the drugs are highly addictive. This means that larger and larger amounts are required to produce the same effect, and when accustomed to their use, the body demands that the supply be continued!

Non-Addictive Psychedelics

These substances under consideration -- peyote and its derivative, mescaline, and LSD -- have been found to be non-addictive. In fact, Dr. Duncan Blewett, psychologist, of the University of Saskatchewan, who has had much experience in this field, says that these preparations can not possibly do any harm, and that they may be of inestimable value to many people; that they are "as harmless as salt"!

A personal friend of mine was one of several investigators sent out independently of each other by a U.S. agency to study the use of peyote by the Indians in various areas. He states that these investigators were unanimous in their reports that they found no addictive or physiologically harmful effects. Those deprived of it showed no withdrawal symptoms, nor any physiological craving. In our own experiments, we have found that a much smaller dose is effective in those who have had it previously, which is the opposite of the situation found with such addictive drugs as opium.

In the religious use of peyote by the American Indians, it is apparently available to all of the worshippers, and participants, including Dr. Humphrey Osmond, have reported it as usually an all-night ceremony. In ancient Egypt, however, the sacred mushroom was carefully guarded by the priests for their own use. Perhaps the guarding was in order to maintain the priestly power and prestige; for it sometimes happens that after taking one of these substances, psychic powers are enhanced.

The effects on the mind, produced by all of these psychedelics, seems quite similar; although exact effects depend, like those of most medications, on the condition of the participant or patient. Each individual is just that, an individual. The chemistry of bodies differs, one from another, and even in the same individual, from one time to another. The mental and emotional status of persons also affects the reactions produced by these chemicals. Dr. Osmond says that they merely "open a door" into the deeper levels of the mind, and that what one finds there depends on the individual.

12

WHY
PSYCHEDELICS?

Psychedelics are members of a class of materials which affect the state of consciousness. The word means "consciousness-expanding" or "mind-manifesting". These substances have been known, in natural form, since before recorded history, as certain mushrooms, cactus "buttons", seeds, etc. The newness is only in the form of some of the synthetic chemicals, such as lysergic acid

There seems to be little or no evidence of physiological damage from these substances. They are not narcotic, addictive or habit-forming.

diethylamide (LSD) or psilocybin. They have been used in the spiritual exercises of various religious groups, both ancient and modern, to assist man to reveal his Mind to himself, and to help him reach heightened levels of awareness.

A Tool

A psychedelic substance is a tool which, when properly used, can open a door to new levels of awareness and perception. However, like all tools, it can be used improperly; none can be used indiscriminately, or for all purposes. There is an art to use. A Stradivarius violin may be a superb musical instrument, but one who does not know how to play a violin is likely to be much disappointed in the sounds which he obtains from it!

Just so, the psychedelics should not be judged on the basis of a single experience, or even a few experiences, especially if these have been taken in a purely experimental frame of mind. The purpose with which the subject submits himself to the experience, the way in which he prepares himself for it, the setting within which he takes it, and the help of a sympathetic guide or monitor who has himself had the experience, all will have tremendous influence on the results.

Opens Doors

When a psychedelic is used to open the "door" that separates the conscious mind from the unconscious, the result may at first be overwhelming. New feelings and perceptions come flooding in. If one tries to cope with these by rationalizing them, and fitting them into his old conceptual framework, he may be thrown into an uncomfortable state of confusion; the intellectual processes may be swamped, and the attempts to establish order fail. However, this frightening and distressing state disappears as one becomes willing to relinquish the old concepts and to experience himself and his world in a new and unaccustomed manner. Support and guidance of a monitor who has himself established some order in this world of un-habitual perceptions can be very important at this stage.

The subject may also develop an acute awareness of the feelings and unspoken throughts of others. This strikes him as so unusual that he may conclude that others present can read his thoughts and that he is, so to speak, psychologically naked. Any distrust of others may become magnified into a paranoidal sort of suspicion and anxiety. This may be minimized by prior establishment of rapport with the monitor, and with any others who are to be present.

None of these unpleasant episodes is necessary when one has learned the proper approach to the experience. The strait to be crossed in moving into the state of expanded consciousness may initially prove to be a rather rough and storm-tossed ride, particularly for a highly controlled and intellectual personality. Later, with more familiarity with these realms of experience, the passage may become smooth and pleasurable.

The subject may enter then upon a succession of hallucinatory experiences. Brilliantly colored geometrical patterns may present a constantly changing spectacle of aesthetic delight. It is as though the ego, having lost the battle to divert attention through unpleasantness, seeks to charm and distract the conscious mind by throwing up a smoke screen of hallucinations to hide the inner Reality which it fears. The visions may portray scenes and inelude incidents as in a technicolor dream, or they may be more symbolic and fraught with meaning. They may convey a representation of one's specific approach to life, or the insight may be more general, and of a philosophical-religious nature. The subject may feel strongly that "We are all One", with a greatly intensified awareness of relationship with others and with the Universe. With seemingly endless variety, the unconscious mind employs visual and other symbolic representations to instruct the conscious mind in what it needs to know!

Gradually the subject may come to see and accept himself, not as an individual with "good" and "bad" characteristics, but as one who simply is. By relinquishing his concepts and surrendering himself to the experience, he finds he can move beyond the state where Reality is symbolic, to a totally new condition in which it is experienced directly.

Levels of Consciousness

So the psychosomatic symptoms, the model psychoses, the multi-colored hallucinatory images, tend to disappear. The individual develops an awareness of aspects of Reality

other than those to which he is accustomed. He knows by direct experience that this deeper Reality, which he apprehends directly, is really there; he is as certain of this as he is of his own existence! He perceives what he may attempt to describe as "levels" of consciousness, or "other dimensions" of space. But he can no more describe these than one who is in love can describe this experience to one who has never been in love.

Above all, he comes to experience himself in a totally new way, and finds that the age-old question, "Who am I?"does have a significant answer. He experiences himself as a far greater being than he had ever imagined, while at the same time his conscious self

Consciousness is not thinking, nor is it dependent upon words or symbols. I could see, I could feel, I could know!

(as conceived up to this point) appears as a far smaller fraction of the whole than he had realized. Further, he sees that his own self is by no means so separate from other selves as he might have thought. Nor is he separate from the universe about him!

These realizations, while not new to mankind, or possibly not new to the subject intellectually, may be very new in an experiential sense. And so they make for altered behavior. The individual sees clearly that some of his actions are not in line with his new knowledge, and that changes are obviously called for. Behavior patterns, established by many years of usage, are not easily or quickly changed. Nevertheless, because the individual's new knowledge of himself is based on direct experience, his behavior does tend to change, and to become more appropriate to his expanded picture of himself.

The English poet-scientist, Edward Carpenter, writing some half-century ago, has described this well.

> *"Of all the hard facts of science, I know of none more solid and fundamental than the fact that, if you inhibit thought (and persevere) you come at length to a region of consciousness below or behind thought, and different from ordinary thought in its nature and charac-*

ter—a consciousness of quasi-universal quality,
and a realization of an altogether vaster Self
than that to which we are accustomed. And
since the ordinary consciousness, with which
we are concerned in ordinary life, is before all
things founded on the little local self, and is in
fact self-consciousness in the little local sense, it
follows that to pass out of that is to die to the
ordinary self, and the ordinary world."

This experience is breathtakingly and wonderfully new, whatever the individual's previously held beliefs, religious or non-religious, may have been. The direct perception of one's Self as an indestructible Self, rather than a destructible ego, may bring the most profound reorientation at the deepest level of the personality. The individual sees that anxiety over anything whatsoever is inappropriate to this new awareness of his transcendental nature. Hostility in any form is likewise uncalled for, since in essence he is one with all mankind and with all the universe. Guilt is a denial of his essential nature and is so seen. From all such negative responses to life he begins to feel free. As it is stated in the Upanishads, "Having realized his self as the Self, a man becomes selfless; and in virtue of selflessness he is to be conceived as unconditioned. This is the highest mystery, betokening emancipation."

Thus there is nothing new in "consciousness expansion". Men have, through the ages and in all cultures, discovered various techniques and disciplines for increasing the accessibility of the "other side" of consciousness, and have also discovered the conditions of attitude and character a man must meet if he wishes to continue to grow in knowledge of his higher Self.

The psychedelics provide only one route through to this "other side" of consciousness; they, with other methods, can enable one to see more clearly what conditions must be met in order to realize this Self. They do not remove or short-cut those conditions. As Aldous Huxley puts it in his *The Perennial Philosophy,*

> *"The nature of this one Reality is such that it can not be directly and immediately apprehended except by those who have chosen to fulfill certain conditions, making themselves loving, pure in heart, and poor in spirit, why should this be so ? We do not know. It is just one of those facts which we have to accept, whether we like them or not, and however implausible and unlikely they may seem. Nothing in our everyday experience gives us any reason for supposing that water is made up of hydrogen and oxygen; and yet, when we subject water to certain rather drastic treatments, the nature of its constituent elements becomes manifest.*
>
> *Similarly, nothing in our everyday experience gives us much reason for supposing that the mind of the average sensual man has, as one of its constituents, something resembling, or identical with, the Reality substantial to the manifold world; and yet, when that mind is subjected to certain rather drastic treatments, the divine element, of which it is at least in part composed, becomes manifest, not only to the mind itself, but also, by its reflection in external behavior, to other minds. It is*

only by making physical experiments that we can discover the intimate nature of matter and its potentialities.   And it is only by making psychological and moral experiments that we can discover the intimate nature of mind, and its potentialities. In the ordinary circumstances of average sensual life, these potentialities of the mind remain latent and unmanifested. If we would realize them, We must fulfill certain conditions and obey certain rules which experience has shown empirically to be valid."

The possibilities of the psychedelic substances are exciting, since they can provide access by many to realms of consciousness which have hitherto been available only to a few. The real frontier today is not outer space, but "inner space" - man's inner Being or consciousness. The psychedelics can be very efficient "space vehicles"!

Psychedelics Help Beginners

There is much interest at present in psychedelic substances for helping beginners to find the reality of mystical experience, helping them to gain insight, and understanding of their inner Selves. These preparations include peyote, a southwestern cactus, mescaline (a derivative of peyote), and lysergic acid diethylamide (LSD). These substances seem to produce a dissociation of consciousness from the usual physical centering, and to bring about an awareness of a more inclusive Reality. Because it is a good description of a typical reaction, and because it gives some glimpse into what we refer to as "mystical experience", I quote what one experimenter reported:

"As the drug takes effect, one appears to an outside observer to be lethargic, perhaps even asleep, but this is far from being the case, for he is going through what is probably the most remarkable experience of his Ufe! For during this stage, when one appears to be sleeping, comes that experience called by mystics 'the realization of the God within us'. This comes to many under these drugs, and is an indescribable, piercing,-beautiful knowing, which goes beyond the body, the mind, the reason, theintellect, into an area of pure knowing. One sees that body, mind, reason, intellect, etc., are all man-made concepts, with very little relation to Reality. It is an inwardly sure knowing. There is no sensation of time. God is no longer only 'out there' somewhere, but He is within you, and you are one with Him. No doubt of it even crosses one's awareness at this stage. You are beyond the knower and the known, where there is no duality, but only oneness and unity, and great love. You not only see truth, but you are Truth. You are Love. You are all things! It is not an ego-inflating experience, but on the contrary, one which can help to dissolve the ego. **Reality was Mind, and Mind was Reality. The formed and the formless are the same. Unity and diversity are the same. Reality is One, and Many, and beyond both the One and the Many!** *It gives one a splendid flash of what can be, and what one must surely aim for. It resolves the goal, and the goal is found most wor-*

thy of pursuit. The consciousness or awareness is expanded far beyond that of the normal state. And this level of consciousness, which actually is available to us at all times, is found to be that part of us which, for want of a better way to express it, might be called the 'God-ness' of us. We find that this God-ness is unchangeable and indestructible, and that its foundation is Love, in its purest form.

"The uninitiated complain that what one experiences under these conditions is merely hallucination. But, once having experienced this or something similar, you know beyond any doubt that you have made immediate and direct contact with God within you. No discussion or argument or criticism by anyone or group, no matter how learned they may be, can ever dissuade you. You begin to realize, even in normal consciousness, that the daily life you lead is needlessly fraught with frustrations, anxieties, problems, worries, all the things which go to make life a really dreary round of futility; but with just a very little shift in values, and a little effort, the daily duties of what we call life can be performed with equanimity, while the Inner Self remains calm and serene, even in the face of apparent disaster. Utilizing this Inner Self as the working basis of your life, you realize fully that nothing can ever hurt you or bother you, not even death. It gives life a completely new meaning, and one which is indestructible, and which fits in with the scheme of things. You no

longer find yourself an outsider, separated from Nature and separated from God, and separated from fellow beings. Frankly, I prefer this 'hallucination' to the one perpetrated by our 'normal' fellows!"

As you may see, this induced mystical experience can open a door to understanding for many. It is not a shortcut but, as one experimenter said, "It has proved beyond any shadow of a doubt the reality of Spirit, of God. And now I am willing to earn, by way of effort, the right to live in this Reality."

Those who are interested in the achievement of mystical experience will find much help in the practice of the various techniques of concentration, meditation and contemplation, which have been developed by both Western and Eastern seekers. There are many books which, if understood, can be guides and helps to finding "the little gate"—to pass

It was not "I" that was being aware of things, but it was simply an awareness of awareness, in which the sense of "I" was no longer functioning.

through which we must discard or transmute the ego or lower self. In reading these books, one must have the eye of the spirit open at least to some extent, in order to realize meanings which are beyond the obvious. For mystical experience can not be expressed in words, any more than can the flavor of a strawberry; we can say only that it tastes like a strawberry!

Each one must begin where he is. The door at which "I" stand and knock is in our hearts. We begin to open the door when we begin to cleanse ourselves of self, of ego, of selfishness, and begin a little to live as our Higher Self; when we change the center of our consciousness from the body to the mind, and then on to center in the Spirit, the Self, the Christ, so that it is no longer "i" (ego, selfishness), but "I (Christ) who lives in me. Only you can do this for yourself. Only you can open the door, and place your feet upon the Path. May you go in Love and Peace!

13

RELIGION & CHEMISTRY

The mystical experience is often considered the greatest goal of human life and the true, though often unrecognized, purpose of all religion. By "mystical experience" is meant here a state of consciousness in which the individual finds his one-ness with the Universe, and in which he feels unconditional love for his earthly brothers and his heavenly Father. In Eastern terminology

These concepts, including the Highest, are experiences in our own consciousness.

this is called "Self-Realization"—the discovery, the making real in our lives, of our true spiritual Self. The Christian may call it a "vital experience of God", "coming to know Christ",—or a "creative integration" of the personality around the deep center. Religious ceremonies, creeds and sacraments have value only as they help man to find this personal relationship with the Infinite, and in doing so to realize his true Self. Chemistry may now provide an effective aid to the achievement of this experience.

The Secret Path

The way to the mystic state of consciousness is often referred to as "The Secret Path". The path is not really secret, although it certainly is not obvious. The Buddha said that it is as "narrow as a razor's edge". It is over this difficult Path, propelled by great faith and strong wills, that all the mystics have traveled, to experience God, or Reality, rather than just to believe in its existence.

Today there are many seeking for the path, but who are too shaken by the pace of modern life to muster the faith and the will necessary to tread this "razor's edge". For such, there is now available the aid of the psychedelic (meaning consciousness-expanding) chemicals—which literally may be a God-send. Through the effects of these chemicals, many may be granted a glimpse of the wonderful world of Reality, where oneness rather than separate-ness is the normal way of life; where Love is the law, and all live thereby. One experimenter, an atheist, after his first psychedelic experience, said, I have seen God! I know that Reality is there, that it is desirable above all things, and that it is attainable. Now I am willing to take the path of effort, to earn the right to have and to keep this Reality. I know now that I, too, may become the Way, the Truth and the Life!"

Modern chemistry has produced many compounds which modify the mind of man by changing the chemistry of the body. Tranquilizers, chemicals which relieve tensions, neuroses, and even psychoses, are well known. The psychedelics, however, when properly used have a more constructive effect in that they may produce understanding, and thus, unlike the tranquilizers, can remove the cause of the tensions—occasionally in a single dose! Thus they can have the unusual effect of opening wider the "doors of perception" to Self-Understanding. On the physical level they enable one to see with new vision and to hear with new understanding. On a higher level, they can develop our awareness of spiritual Reality which, the masters have told us, is the Real world.

Many substances, including opium, hashish and alcohol, have been used in an attempt to find a shortcut to wisdom. These are likely to disappoint the user because the "awareness" is usually of very inferior quality. Also, some of these are highly addictive, which means that larger and larger amounts are required to produce an effect—and when accustomed to their use, the body demands that the supply be continued.

Psychedelics

Fortunately there are psychedelic, or consciousness-expanding, substances which are not addictive. Among these is peyote, a form of cactus used for centuries by the American Indians. A personal friend was one of the several investigators sent out by the federal government to study the use of peyote by Indians in various areas. He reported that the investigators were unanimous in finding no evidence of either physiological or psychological harm from this use of peyote. Peyote is not considered addictive by the Narcotics Bureau.

Other psychedelic substances, produced by modern chemistry, include mescaline, LSD and psilocybin. Mescaline is the active substance found in peyote; LSD is a derivative of ergot, a fungus growing on grain; and psilocybin is derived from a species of mushroom growing in Mexico.

Supportive Guidance

It is very important that the psychedelic approach to the mystical or religious experience be under sympathetic and supportive guidance. As with any chemical—or food!—there is always a possibility of undesirable side-effects. Physiologically, in their effects on the body, the psychedelics have been described by one investigator as being "as safe as aspirin"—which, of course, if wrongly used can be quite harmful. There is nothing so harmless that harm can not be done with it by stupid or malicious persons! Psychologically, it is possible for harm to follow the improper use of psychedelics, due to the occasional ventilation of repressed materials from the subconscious, unless proper guidance is available at the time.

As the experience is usually conducted, the psychedelic substance is given in the morning, the subject having eaten nothing since the previous evening. After an hour or so, some nausea and vertigo may be noticed, but this usually soon passes. Sometimes there is a period of euphoria, when ordinary things may seem unusually beautiful, or even humorous. However, at the end of three or four hours, most of

All agree that some control is necessary, but it seems important that their use for religious purposes be protected.

the participants, if properly guided, will wish to be quiet and to look within their own consciousness, to find the inner Self. Some enjoy music, or flowers, or pictures, for these frequently take on extraordinary qualities, and very often aid the subject in going into the deeper levels of awareness.

Meaning of Life

Life and Love are usually experienced as everywhere present. One seems to have a new understanding of the meaning and purpose of life, and a new awareness of his own identity as one with the Universe, and of his neighbor as an integral part of himself. It is much easier, during the psychedelic experience, to realize that our true identity is not that of the body or the personality. This is a wonderful lesson, for it is one of the important steps toward the Father's house, away from separateness, and toward Unity—this knowing that I AM, and that "I and my Father are One".

Misunderstood

It is indeed regrettable that the use of these potentially wonderful psychedelic substances is coming to be misunderstood by the public. There seems to be a campaign to lead the public to believe that they are highly addictive and dangerous drugs; and this is leading to repressive legislation. All agree that some control is necessary, but it seems important that their use for religious purposes be protected. In every case where the matter has been brought to court, the American Indians have won the right to continue their use of peyote for religious purposes, and one can hope for the same rights for the white man.

The use of herbs to promote religious experience can be traced back through thousands of years, for the psychedelics, like penicillin, were originally a gift of Nature. The "sacred mushroom" of ancient Egypt, eaten ceremonially by the priests to stimulate psychic ability and mystical experience, was psychedelic or consciousness-expanding; and a species of mushroom is still used in Mexico in the search for enlightenment. Peyote, a cactus, is used by the American Indians—and by some of the newer Americans! The Hindu scriptures mention a plant called Soma, and modern African natives have been found to use a plant called Daga for similar purposes. The fact that our body chemistry does affect not only our physical nature but also our mental and spiritual perceptions has been recognized for thousands of years.

No one can predict what results a given individual may expect from a psychedelic experience. The consciousness-expanding effect does not add anything to the mind, but seems to open the way for our discovery of our own Inner Self. Dr. Humphry Osmond, Director of the New Jersey Neuro-Psychiatric Institute, at Princeton, reports from his long work in this field that the psychedelics merely open a door to another level of consciousness within a person, and that what is found when that door is opened depends upon what is already there. His little couplet, written some years ago in a letter to Aldous Huxley, gave the name to these substances:

"To fall in hell, or soar angelic,
Just take a pinch of psychedelic!"

It is possible to fall in hell—to have a quite disturbing psychedelic experience. So much depends upon the purpose and nature of the person undertaking it, and the setting for the experience itself. If one is truly seeking the Highest, then the psychedelic experience can be of great help. If one is merely curious, then he will probably find little; if potentially psychotic, then there can be great dangers involved, unless the experience is conducted under adequate supervision.

When subjects are chosen carefully for this experience, the results are usually rewarding. Each experience is unique,

for each individual is different from every other person. And since even—the same person is different at different times, so he may have a variety of psychedelic experiences. This experience can open a door to understanding for many. It can prove beyond a shadow of doubt, by one's own experience, the nature of Reality. It can stimulate us then to build, and earn by our own efforts, the right to live always in this Reality.

To have, even for a day, a look at ourselves and at our world from a new perspective is an experience likely never to be forgotten, and probably a major stimulus to our spiritual growth. To learn that our emotions, and even our religious insights, may be affected by chemistry should not detract from the value,—for is not chemistry also of God?

By "psychedelic experience" is meant the experience of a change in consciousness or awareness induced by chemicals. The word "psychedelic" means "consciousness-expanding" or "mind manifesting", and the substances used for this purpose include mescaline, peyote, LSD, psilocybin, certain species of mushrooms, morning glory seeds, and a number of others less well-known.

Considerable confusion seems to exist in the mind of the public regarding the use of psychedelics. This is the result of several factors, an important one being the lack of real knowledge of the subject by many who write about it for public consumption. There is also the further fact that these substances are used for purposes other than psychedelic—such as the treatment of the mentally ill, the treatment of alcoholism, and use by juveniles who may take them Just for kicks."

To an outside observer, a subject in a psychedelic experience may appear to be in a condition resembling, in some ways, alcoholic intoxication; the one who has taken the chemical may make some very strange statements, such as "being one with everything", "experiencing God", or "knowing all things". Or he may speak of being apart from his body, or of an awareness that he really is neither that body, nor the personality which goes under his name! Anyone with an understanding of the mystical experience or "cosmic consciousness" would immediately recognize what is meant by such statements, but they are grossly misunderstood by the public.

Questions

The first question, in dealing with the subject of psyche-delics is, "Is, or is not, consciousness really 'expanded'?" Is it true that new insights and a new understanding of life are developed as a result of this experience? Many articles have been written to prove the negative—that there is no expansion of awareness, no change for the better in those who have had the experience. One entire book was written with this objective—but was based on a single experience by the author, which he had under very unfavorable cir-cumstances!

The testimony of those who have worked for years with these substances, and of a large percentage of the subjects who have had the experience, is positive. Consciousness is expanded; new insights are gained. New understanding of other people and love for them does develop. And the problems of life are very often recognized as opportunities for growth. It has also been reported that about 40% of alcoholics who have failed to benefit by any other type of treatment have been salvaged, in some cases after only one properly oriented psychedelic experience!

A major difficulty in evaluating this "expanded" consciousness is that there are no words which can be used to describe it to one who has not experienced it. How could you describe the color red—or any color!—to a person who had been born blind! And because of this lack of real communication, there is a considerable prejudice against accepting the value of the mystical experience, and just as the religious mystics seem never to have been popular with the orthodoxly religious—because they speak of experiencing God, and not just of "believing in" God, so those who have had a chemically induced expansion of awareness are never likely to be understood by the mass of people who have little interest in this type of experience.

A second important question deals with the possible dangers inherent in the experience. One newspaper article told of how an elephant had been killed by a single dose of LSD; and it added, "Some people are foolish enough to take these drugs !" About half of the subjects taking mescaline or peyote do have mildly unpleasant side-effects, such as nausea, or some degree of anxiety. The latter often because new sensations are being experienced, and we are all likely to be a little apprehensive of that with which we are unfamiliar. The incidence of nausea is much less with LSD, but anxiety is probably as common. There seems to be little or no evidence of physiological damage from these substances. They are not narcotic, addictive or habit-forming.

Psychological damage, however, is possible—just as it is from any life experience. One investigator reported two suicides in some 5,000 cases of the drug experience—

The chemical itself is only a "trigger". If the trigger falls on an unloaded chamber, there will be no explosion, no expansion;

to which one psychiatrist commented that this made the psychedelic experience much safer than ordinary psychotherapy! And certainly they seem infinitely safer than alcohol or tobacco, both of which are found to be directly responsible for a staggering number of cases of illness and death! These latter, being financially profitable, and protected by vast commercial interests, is it not possible that we have been "brain-washed" into disregarding their dangers? The psychedelics could be a threat to these interests, because of the new insights which are so often developed!

The testimony of researchers is that there is no more possibility of harmful results than in almost any life experience one can mention. Certainly it seems safer to have a psychedelic experience than it is to ride in a car, or a train, or an airplane!

Although there seems to be no physiological addiction to these substances, the desire of many who appear to lack growth-motivation to return as often as possible to the chemically-induced state seems to pose a problem. Daily use is reported by a few college students. Perhaps we might compare this to students of music who neglect to practice on their instruments because they are so enthralled with listening to records of their favorite musicians. They experience great enjoyment, but in the meantime are developing no competence as musicians. To actualize our own inner potential is the purpose of life. It would seem that the chemical experience itself, no matter how often repeated, will not bring this result. But if it is used with caution, and with understanding, an occasional chemical experience can be a useful stimulus to growth.

Spiritual Rebirth

The psychedelic experience has been interestingly compared with obstetrics. To monitor a subject who is having a psychedelic experience is to practice "spiritual obstetrics", for in so many cases it seems that one is helping to "deliver" a materially-oriented spirit to a new world of light,—assisting in a spiritual re-birth. It is, of course, true that there are some stillbirths in both forms of obstetrics, and in some cases the labour is long and difficult. But the occurrence of such reactions has never been considered a contraindication for pregnancy! Most parents, and most

spiritual aspirants, seem to feel that the possible gains far outweigh any element of risk—which can be minimized by skilled supervision in either category.

It could be most unfortunate if this form of "spiritual obstetrics" should come completely under the control of the medical profession—just as it is unfortunate that childbirth has lost many of its spiritual values by being regarded as almost entirely a medical incident. When the psychedelics are used in a purely medical manner, there is likely to be little of spiritual value obtained. There is likely to be a high incidence of hallucinations, and perhaps even the activation of some potential psychoses—though of course the latter could be of great therapeutic value if the patient is under adequate professional care. But when the experience is oriented toward increased spiritual growth, in peaceful surroundings, and especially when there is good rapport with the monitor, there will result a maximum incidence of "consciousness-expansion" or "mystical experience". Many who are using them in this way estimate that about 75% have some degree of consciousness expansion, of which better than a third have been truly remarkable experiences, and that the incidence of any harmful reaction is very low, though always possible.

In a democratic society, all minorities are subject to control by the majority, even though that control is exercised in ignorance of the problems faced by the minorities. In the long run, no doubt this is good, for it forces the minority groups to demonstrate to the very best of their ability the worth of that for which they stand. So while we may resent the criticisms broadcast by those ignorant of the psychedelics, these very criticisms can be a factor in improving and increasing the value of our psychedelic research.

In summary, then, experience with these chemicals-indicates that this expanded awareness, when spiritually-oriented, can, and in a majority of cases does, result in the development of new insights, new understanding of the self and its relationships with the world, and a new love for God and neighbor. The dangers are minimal when the subjects are in an environment of love and support; and under such conditions, new doors of awareness, to new levels of consciousness can most certainly be opened for those who are ready. It should be remembered, however, that the chemical itself is only a "trigger". If the trigger falls on an unloaded chamber, there will be no explosion, no expansion; and even if it falls on a loaded chamber, the explosion can be dangerous if the "gun" is not properly aimed.

The experience might be compared to the tow which is given to a glider to get it into the air. Most gliders would never leave the ground without this assistance. But, once in the air, if the glider is airworthy, and the pilot capable, the flight can be most exhilarating!

14

PSYCHEDELICS SHOW THE WAY

The role of psychedelics is often misunderstood. Many feel that having had wonderful experiences, they now have the answers and are somehow changed. And no doubt in many respects they are. But users often overlook the fact that there are usually heavy walls of conditioning and ignorance separating the surface mind from the core of our being. It is a blessing that psychedelics can set aside these barriers and give access to our real Self. But unless one is committed to the changes indicated, old habits of personality can rapidly reestablish themselves.

At this point many feel that repeating the experience will maintain the exalted state. It may, but most often real change requires hard work and dedicated effort. Unfortunately this is not always clear during the experience itself; it has merely pointed the way and shown what is possible. If we like what we see, it is now up to us to bring about the changes indicated.

There is a grace period following profound psychedelic experiences when changes can be rapidly made. At this time one is infused with the wonder and power of the new information. Moreover—and this is an area where some valuable research can be done—the drug experience releases a great deal of bodily and psychic armoring that is tied to our neuroses. This rejuvenation is quite noticeable after a good psychedelic experience, when, without the dragging weight of physical habit patterns, behavior can be more readily changed.

On the other hand, if you make no effort to change, old habits rapidly reassert themselves, and you find yourself sliding back into your previous state. In fact, it can be worse than before, because now you know that things can be better and are disappointed to find yourself mucking around in the same old garbage.

Another factor makes this process even more uncomfortable. A lot of the energy formerly tied up in repressed material is now released. This energy may be used quite fruitfully to expand the boundaries of your being to the new dimensions you have experienced. But if you return to old patterns of behavior, you now have more energy to reinforce them, making life more difficult. For this reason, these experiences must not be taken lightly, but with serious intent.

Set and Setting

Set and setting have been widely recognized as the two most important factors in undertaking a psychedelic experience. Of these, set has the greatest influence.

As the drug opens the door to the unconscious, huge spectrums of possibilities of experience present themselves. Just how one steers through this vast maze depends mostly upon set. Set includes the contents of the personal unconscious, which is essentially the record of all one's life experience. It also includes one's walls of conditioning, which determine the freedom with which one can move through various vistas. Another important aspect of set consists of one's values, attitudes, and aspirations. These will influence the direction of attention and determine how one will deal with the psychic material encountered.

In fact, one can learn a great deal by accepting and reconciling oneself with uncomfortable material. Resisting this discomfort, on the other hand, can greatly intensify the level of pain, leading to disturbing, unsatisfactory experiences, or even psychotic attempts at escape. This latter dynamic is largely responsible for the medical profession's view of these materials as psychotomimetic. On the other hand, surrender, acceptance, gratitude, and appreciation can result in continual opening, expansion, and fulfillment.

Setting, or the environment in which the experience takes place, can also greatly influence the experience, since subjects are often very suggestible under psychedelics. Inspiring ritual, a beautiful natural setting, stimulating artwork, and interesting objects to examine can focus one's attention on rewarding areas. Most important of all is an experienced, compassionate guide who is very familiar with the process. His mere presence establishes a stable energy field that helps the subject remain centered. The guide can be very helpful should the subject get stuck in uncomfortable places, and can ask intelligent questions that will help resolve difficulties, as well as suggesting fruitful directions of exploration that the subject might have otherwise overlooked. The user will also find that simply sharing what is happening with an understanding listener will produce greater clarity and comfort. Finally, a good companion knows that the best guide is one's own inner being, which should not be interfered with unless help is genuinely needed and sought.

From *Journal of Borderland Research* Vol.19, No. 6 ,
September 1963, by permission

PART II
TRIPPING WITH GOD

From *Fate*, Vol. 16, No. 5, May, 1963, by permission.

15

FINDING GOD BY PILL

Abrief description of a typical psychedelic reaction may be of interest. The material is best taken in the morning, with no food since the previous evening. After a period of thirty minutes to an hour, one may feel slightly light-headed. Some experience nausea, which is usually not severe, and passes away within an hour or so. Other physiological symptoms likely to develop are a slowing of the heart rate and the rate of breathing, a decrease in blood pressure, dilating of the pupils of the eyes, and a peripheral vasoconstriction which causes most subjects to feel cold.

> *There may be a loss of touch with the usual concepts of the world around, together with changes in the concept of the self.*

During the second hour, there may be a loss of touch with the usual concepts of the world around, together with changes in the concept of the self. There may also be symptoms of lethargy and apathy, and occasionally confusion. There is sometimes a period of euphoria and ordinary things may seem inordinately funny.

By the time two or three hours have elapsed, most of the participants want to be quiet, and to look within their own consciousness. Some enjoy music, or studying flowers or pictures. The enjoyment of these things is not at all at the intellectual level, but they are seen from a new level of consciousness, from which the subject feels that he actually is the music or the flower, or the picture. Ordinary objects become most extraordinary in appearance, as a result of our new appreciation of their "reality". Life and love are seen everywhere, and one seems to have new understanding of life, its meaning and purpose, and a new awareness of his own identity as "one with the universe", or "one with God", and of his neighbor as an integral part of himself. It is much easier, in the psychedelic experience, to realize that our true identity is not that of the body-mind-emotions complex which is designated by our name. To have this experience, to know that I AM, and "I and my Father are one", is a most salutary one; for it is a first step toward our Father's house, away from separateness, and toward unity.

Ordinary objects become most extraordinary in appearance.

Our own experiments have been conducted with a view to finding the highest possible level of consciousness, and to achieve the "oneness" of which all mystics speak. This seems to be the way in which the Indians use peyote. Anyone who has taken it would realize that the "orgies" reported by some opponents of the experience would be completely impossible. Those whom I have seen have wanted only to be alone, and to seek their souls in solitude and quietness.

However, these potentially very useful and wonderful substances may be misunderstood by the American public as a result of their association with various narcotics in newspaper reports of their use by juvenile delinquent groups. These children are reported to be taking them just for "kicks", and to change from morphine, to barbiturates, to marihuana, to psychedelics. Actually, the latter are the only non-harmful preparations in this list! I have been able to find no reports of harm resulting from the use of the psychedelics by normal people. Their use with psychotics, of course, should be limited to those experienced in dealing with the mentally ill.

It seems that a campaign is being waged against these preparations, and an attempt being made to lead the public to believe that the psychedelics are dangerous and addictive drugs. The State of California has recently declared the use or administration of peyote to be a criminal offense!

Misunderstanding

If this misunderstanding should spread to other states, and be extended to other psychedelics, many people would thereby be denied access to one of the most remarkable experiences possible to humans—a glimpse of a higher level of consciousness, from which one may realize that the universe is founded on Love, that God truly is Love, and that we are made in his Image. This, of course, can be discovered in other ways, but they are difficult and unattractive to Western man, who resents any discipline or effort in his half-hearted search for Truth. A glimpse of this Reality in a psychedelic experience, however, is very likely to convince him that it is truly worth the effort to earn the right, by discipline and effort, to achieve this level and to maintain it as his normal level of consciousness.

It has been speculated by some students of mysticism who are also aware of the psychedelic experience that perhaps the relatively large number of mystics who appeared in the Middle Ages may have been partly the result of their being exposed to the natural form of LSD by eating rye bread contaminated with ergot. Another possibility is that the body chemistry may have been similarly modified by fasting, which was a common practise then, and by the frequent ill-health suffered by those who were convinced of the unimportance of the physical body.

There are those who object strenuously to "finding God" by taking a pill. But all of those who have found God, as a personal or mystical experience, have done something to bring about this longed-for condition of consciousness. Some have fasted; others have imposed various ascetic disciplines; others have used techniques of breathing; and in many cases these techniques have been carried out faithfully for years before the desired affects appears. If we can bring about a similar state, even temporarily, by using chemicals, who is to say that this is an inferior method? Is not chemistry also of God? Few insist on crossing the continent on foot today because jet travel is "unnatural"!

The great Teachers have told us that God is Love, and that we also are Love in our basic essence, but we have failed to understand or to believe. A few of our Eastern brothers have followed the path of fasting and discipline, and have found spiritual enlightenment. They have achieved "oneness with God", or the realization "That art Thou". This realization is the finding of our true Self.

It is an awareness that the basic essence of man is truly the same as the underlying Reality of the universe, which western man calls God.

Those who have walked this secret Path -- "secret" only because there are few who have chosen to find it -- have reported the attainment of peace, bliss, awareness of Reality they have been unable to describe in terms which make sense to ordinary mortals. They have been able to say only, with the Psalmist, "Come, taste and see that the Lord [10] is good!" These have been the mystics who have experienced God as a reality, rather than as a belief. They have never been in favor with orthodoxy, either of science or of religion, because they follow no rules, ceremonies or rituals, so loved by the orthodox. They follow only the Law of Love, and find their only authority within their own hearts, their own consciousness. They listen only to the "still, small voice". They walk in the radiance of the Inner Light, and have need of no other.

Great faith, however, is required to enable one to begin to walk this path. Results, though sure, are slow in coming, and few will persist long enough to feel the quickening of the Spirit within. We of the West want short courses, condensed books, plants of Jack's beanstalk variety which come up quickly -- forgetting that they as quickly wither because they have not depth of root!

Wonderful World of the Spirit

For those of little faith and weak will, the psychedelics may literally be a God-send. Through these chemicals they may be granted a glimpse of this wonderful world of the Spirit, where oneness rather than separation and isolation is the normal way of life; where Love is the Law and all live thereby. One experimenter said, gratefully, after his first psychedelic experience, "I have seen God! I know that Reality is there; that it is desirable above all things; and that is it attainable. Now I am willing to take the path of effort, to earn the right to have and to keep this Reality."

Another participant wrote as follows: "I had a tremendous feeling of being -- not being something, but just being. There was a feeling of oneness with everything. It felt that at last I was 'home' and I felt that it was so wonderful to be 'home'. Then I knew that all the sacred scriptures of the world, the Bible, the Vedas, the Gita, the Koran, were fountains of spiritual refreshment that can remind us what it is like 'at home'. I knew that all of man's temple and cathedral building was but an attempt to satisfy a hunger within himself once again to experience this 'being at home'. One hopes to maintain this feeling of oneness and of being at home, but it is not a desire for the drug again. I feel that the chemical is only a tool to show us what is available; it should be like the opening of the door, and not the continual standing in the doorway."

Perhaps we may compare this experience to that of the prodigal son, when, in the midst of his sensual existence, he "came to himself". He caught a glimpse of the security and love, the joy and peace, to be had in his Father's house. Then he arose and began the journey home.

LET THERE BE SIMPLE NATURAL THINGS DURING THE SESSION

Let there be simple, natural things
tocontract during the session;

> hand woven cloth
> uncarved wood
> ancient music
> flowers—growing things
> burning fire
> a touch of eath
> a splash of water
> fruit . . . good bread . . . cheese
> wine
> sacred smoke
> candles
> temple incense
> a warm hand
> anything more than five hundred years old

Of course it is always best to be
secluded with nature.

From *Psychedelic Prayers & Other Meditations*, Timothy Leary, Ronin, 1997.
by permission

16

PSYCHEDELIC MYSTICISM

by Swami Parampanthi

I am recording here some of the experiences which I had during a very wonderful psychedelic experience, under the guidance of an experienced monitor.

First of all, there was the period of preparation, which I think essential for a right experience. I spent the day before in calm meditation, preparing myself physically and mentally for this religious experience.

In the morning, I took the chemical and sat down quietly, waiting for the experience to come. I was calm, but with a sense of high expectancy. I was looking forward to it, not with a desire for anything spectacular, but with an attitude which was essentially reverential; I was looking toward the exploration of the Great Unknown, which is without and within.

What I Experienced

The first changes which I noticed were visual. As I looked at a wall, it was no longer inert substance, but became an intricate pattern of graceful forms, which began to move in perfect symmetry and rhythm. I could see there the whole drama of creation. I could see the movement of love and desire; the upsurge of the spirit; the violence of emotion; the pangs of birth; the anguish of suffering. As my mind became attuned to the Cosmic Force, I could see there the reflection of the calm and collected mind, and the movement of perfect harmony and rhythm. And as I looked, I could see, actually see, the vibrations of different things - the wall, a table, my hand.

I could see the movement of love and desire; the upsurge of the spirit; the violence of emotion.

Then I saw not only one form of a thing, but many forms. As I looked at a glass, I saw not just one, but many patterns of movement. One glass appeared to be many at the same time.

Then I went outside, and saw the clear, beautiful blue sky - but it was no longer an expanse of a single color, but was vibrant with many colors. It had many tones, many tints, many vibrant motions! As I looked at the grass, it was greener, richer. The trees exhibited a beautiful radiance. The colors of all things were intensified. Blue was no longer simply blue, but was profoundly blue; red was no longer simply red, but a shining, red beauty! In everything I could sense the vibrant rhythm of life. Mentally, I could feel this, and physically I could see this.

And then I could see life!—see it multiformed, as my experience moved into different phases. I began to see the many-colored Reality, which is multiharmonious, multidimensional. In one sweep my perception encompassed sound, movement, color, idea and image. The whole thing was opened into the one intricate structure of Being and Flux, which is Creation Itself.

Nature of Consciousness

I noticed another change in my awareness. I realized suddenly that my awareness was far ahead of my words, or even my thoughts. When the monitor asked me to explain the experiences which I was having, I was unable to do it, because my awareness leaped forward, beyond dimension or time, and words could not catch up with it! My awareness was a thousand miles ahead of my words, or even of my thoughts.

Suddenly I realized the nature of consciousness. I realized that consciousness is not thinking, nor is it dependent upon words or symbols. It can experience without "knowing". It can be aware without the intervention of time—which brought a feeling of intemporality. In a flash, in a split second, I could see, I could feel, I could know! There was no beginning of understanding, nor end of understanding, but the whole awareness was instantaneous.

And then some music began, and in it I could sense the finest texture of tone. The tones were no longer inert sound, but they indicated form, and the form indicated an idea. In the music, the tone, the form, the idea and the rhythm all mingled and rolled into one, to produce a profound experience which is indescribable!

As I reflected upon the nature of Reality, I could sense the perfect flow of rhythm. And later, when the monitor read to me some of the writings of the great Sages, especially the Zen masters, the meaning was instantaneously understood. When he was reading about the Void, I became aware of the sheer brilliance of the Void, the sheer strength of this Existence beyond existence. And this awareness

When one can experience this fearlessly, then he can return to the world of sense and of personality, not with rejection but with understanding.

was not of a temporal sort, nor was it an awareness through intellectual understanding. Actually, I saw that Reality was Mind, and Mind was Reality, and that everything—the form and manifestation of Reality, and Reality Itself, which is beyond form—come from the same eternal substratum. In this eternal substratum, manifestation and non-manifestation are the same. The formed and the formless are the same. Unity and diversity are the same. One thing appears as many, and the many appear as One—while in another sense, Reality is One, and Many, and beyond both the One and the Many!

Another realization came to me: the simultaneous sense of the profound and the ludicrous! Suddenly I realized why the Zen masters always combined profundity with a sense of humor. I realized that something is lacking if we have only profundity. We need a sense of humor, of the ludicrous, to make this little world a place of appeal and hope. When all is profound, then life is unbearable; but if profundity is touched with a sense of lighthearted laughter, of eccentricity, then the profundity is bearable, understandable, against the background of human weaknesses and limitations. Man, confronting the Profound, feels lost, overwhelmed. But when Profundity is touched with a sense of the ludicrous, Reality is neither ordinary nor extraordinary; it is neither this nor that, but is a manifestation which encompasses the whole spectrum of creation, and extends infinitely beyond.

I also experienced a sharpened awareness of the non-dimensional world, which is accompanied by a sense of joy and also an element of terror. Suddenly we see the world of form and sense disintegrating. We try to maintain our dimensional world, in order to maintain our sense of "I". To lose the ego can be a terrifying experience to those who are unprepared! But the disappearance of the sense of "I" and the disintegration of the sense world are steps which are essential to spiritual experience. This is "the dark night of the soul".

When one can experience this fearlessly, then he can return to the world of sense and of personality, not with rejection but with understanding. For then he will know that the ego and the sense world are no longer isolated from the Whole, but are simply manifestations of the One Great Power. With the dissolution of the sense of "I" comes the birth of the Universal Self, after which the conflict between cosmos and universe, God and the world, Soul and flesh, disappears—for the world and the ego are seen as parts of the Cosmic Totality.

During this psychedelic experience there was a loss of ego identification. I did not once think of myself as a static ego, viewing the whole universe, but I realized myself as a continuous movement; I was the process of experiencing! It was more an awareness, and in this awareness there was absolutely no sense of "I". It was not "I" that was being aware of things, but it was simply an awareness of awareness, in which the sense of "I" was no longer functioning.

Everything is Alright

There was a continuous sense of exaltation in this experience, a feeling that basically everything is all right. Not because it has to be all right, but because it does not matter whether the world has a teleological end or not. I understood that it is not necessary for us to see, or try to see, a Divine purpose in life. Nor is it necessary for us to deliberately act for the manifestation of the good. For when man is deliberately good, he is no longer good. When he has to look for a Divine purpose, then he is no longer in tune with that Divine purpose! But when he is that Divine purpose, then thinking about it does not arise.

This experience revealed also to me that the quickening of the senses - of sound, smell, touch, vision - leads to the transcendence of the senses. As one goes into the experience, the sense world is intensified; it is more beautiful, magnificent, incredibly diversified. But then consciousness expands vastly beyond this sense world to a point of rest, of stillness, where one is aware only of the pure Void, which is the only Substance.

After this transcending experience, when awareness once more returns to the sense world, this sense world has become magnified, deified. One feels that everything is touched with Divinity! Then one enjoys everything as a manifestation of the Lord, of the Godhead. Nothing is insignificant or lost, but the least tiny bit is seen as a focus of profound significance. Every blade of grass is seen as important as the sun, the star, the galaxy.

And suddenly there is a profound awareness of the purpose and meaning of life, of the naturalness of Essence, and of Essence as the natural flow of creation - and Creation as the natural flow of that Essence. The world is merged into one, and arguments about God versus matter disappear. There is no longer exploration for "something"; no longer any desire to go "places", to understand "things", to explore "meanings". Suddenly everything is understood. Meanings become clear—the search is forgotten—the worry is over—man has come home! He stands transfigured in the presence of Reality! He IS That Reality!

17

THE MOUNTAIN OF AWAKENING

by John W. Aiken

It was an Initiation. Time and place had little significance. As I went into the deeper levels of the Experience, all awareness of space and time ceased, for pure Being is beyond the opposites of Space and Infinity, Time and Eternity. All alike are seen to be the creation of the human intellect, and the mind itself only a tool of Being—though an important tool, within its limitations. In the final ascent of the Mountain of Awakening, all tools, all creations of the mind—even the awareness of Being itself, must be left behind.

Stages

There were stages in the Initiation. First, of course, was the gathering of the participants, who were drawn together naturally, as part of the Great Pattern. And even at this stage, there was an awareness of a deep significance below the apparently casual surface level.

The preparation of the Sacramental Substances was left to Paul, who felt its grave importance, and seemed unable to hurry the process, though he was quite aware of our impatience. But the deep significance of this coming together, perhaps only once in many lifetimes, was not to be destroyed by haste.

Then there was the taking of the Sacrament itself. It seemed on the surface to be the mere swallowing of a chemical, a fragment torn from the natural world. But did not a Brother once say,

The bee was my symbol of oneness with Ultimate Being.

in giving a group of friends a perhaps similar experience, "This is my Body, broken for you; my Blood shed for you"? And now, as then, these fragments of Reality which we swallowed could not be separated from Reality Itself, for Reality is One. And with these fragments, we were absorbed into that Totality-that-is-One, and all sense of separateness, of ego, of personality, evaporated in the Pure Light.

There seemed to be various levels within this House of Reality which we entered—"mansions in the Father's House". First, there was the theme of Being. My symbol was a bee, held by a string which was almost, but not quite, infinitely extensible. The bee would seem to soar into the heavens and be lost to sight, seeming to become one with Infinity, with pure "bee-ness"; but before this could completely happen, he would be brought back by the string. The bee was my symbol of oneness with Ultimate Being—and at the same time, through the string, the symbol of my own apparent separation from that Ultimate. I was eager to escape the restraints that kept me tied to the world of becoming—but there was work to be done in that world before the "silver cord" could be broken. I was the bee, and the cord, and THAT which included both of them. By repetition, it was impressed upon me that while we can realize that we are one with Reality, we can not achieve the ultimate absorption, because we are also our brothers, who are not yet ready to enter Nirvana; not yet ready to become the Clear Light. This is the restraining cord, which ever returns us to the world of becoming, to the world of process, of evolution.

The next stage is more difficult to describe, for it is impossible to reduce a state of consciousness to words; impossible to find words that will convey any meaning to those who have not been there. But I realized, as a fact of experience, that even the concept we call "God" is also a creation of man himself! I had often joked about the fact that, in the beginning God had created man, and that man had been returning the compliment ever since. But here I saw with crystal clarity that "God" is a creation of man! Each man has an array of concepts - his pictures in the gallery of his mind—of objects, events, people, ideas. And in his most carefully guarded inner place, he keeps his Highest Concept, which for him is "God". But all of these concepts, including the Highest, are experiences in his own consciousness.

We recognize the fact that it is impossible for us to know the ultimate nature even of a simple, apparently inanimate object; and knowledge of the ultimate nature of Reality itself is completely out of the question. Modern science attempts to remove the veils which hide the nature of the "precipitated reality"which we call "matter"—and the picture becomes more and more awesome with each subsequent unveiling. But still the picture remains only a mental concept, and not the Reality Itself!

Is it any wonder, then, that the sages have little or nothing to say of the ultimate nature either of man, or of the Totality-that-is-One, in which man is included! Yet most of us need our gallery of concepts, and perhaps especially we need this hidden, secret place, this shrine within which the time-bound soul may renew its awareness of its own Being. We need our self-created Highest Concept—and may it continue to increase in stature and Wisdom! For this is our preparation for leaving this Mansion of Concepts for that higher Mansion-of-no-Concepts, where one is face to face with THAT which transcends all concepts.

Finding a Path up the Mountain

Next, the symbol of the Mountain was used to present another insight. I saw many hundreds of people, working to build a path up the mountain. I saw them working with primitive tools first, carefully moving rocks and replacing them with their hands, to form a usable path. Then a them working with the help of animals. And again, with modern machinery. But always it was with the same problem that they were dealing: building a Path up the Mountain. And I saw that each must build the path for himself, and he must also build it for his brother.

A Way Station

This way station, where the Initiation was given, seemed to be the farthest advanced base-camp on the Mountain. Beyond it was only the bare, wind-swept slope, which led to the top. There was no ceremony of separation, for there was nothing or no one from whom I could be separated!

I was all beings, all consciousness. I was not a separated beam of the Great Radiance; "I" was that Radiance itself! And yet I was limited. There was still duality, in spite of my awareness of non-duality, of Oneness.

As I ascended the last great slope of the Mountain, I knew that every impediment had to go. The little self, the ego, had long since vanished. There was no longer "John" or "Paul", or any other separation by name or form. There was no longer even any concept of "God", for this, too, had to be left behind. There was only consciousness, awareness, and the sharp winds of Eternity, on the top of that mighty peak of Awareness. And the "winds" were also the Clear Radiance, with which all things are illumined. There remained only Awareness—but yet something

As I ascended the last great slope of the Mountain, I knew that every impediment had to go.

else, the last trace of duality, the awareness of Awareness! I knew, however, that the final step was to go forward from that Mountain top, joyfully to become One with the Clear Radiance, and with that final act of renunciation, which was also the final act of Becoming, there would no longer be any "awareness of Awareness", but only Awareness Itself, Nirvana, the Clear Light of the Void.

And yet it was not possible! For the bee, in the earlier symbolism, was bound by the silver cord to the world of becoming; and now I was bound by my awareness of oneness with the many who were still climbing the lower reaches of the Mountain. And I was also one with the multitudes (also I) who were as yet unaware even of the existence of the Mountain. One can not go until all can go, for truly all are One!

I could feel the tremendous implications of the Essence of Being, in that Reality of which nothing can be said - or even thought! There was a yearning to be THAT, and a knowledge of the magnificence of the statement, "THAT ART THOU!" But there was also a call from the valley. For while one part of my consciousness, which was Universal Consciousness, was glimpsing the Clear Light, the other part was yet asleep in the valley, or half-awake in those who were beginning to stir. It is all One, but it must all be awakened, for there is no achievement of Ultimate Being while any part is still held in the relativity of becoming.

Each individual who approaches the door of Nirvana is Universal Consciousness, catching a glimpse of the Ultimate, and by this glimpse, Universal Consciousness becomes expanded. To the extent that each part grows, the whole thereby grows, for each "one", each "part" is ALL!

And so Consciousness returned to the Valley—but Consciousness had expanded, and there was a slight ripple of excitement in the Valley, as a few more became aware of the challenge of the Mountain, and one or two made  ready for the Ascent. And I learned that I am my brother's keeper—because I am my brother!

RETURNING TO THE SOURCE—REPOSE

Be empty
Watch quietly while the ten thousand forms
Swim into life and retun to the source

Do nothing
Return to the source

Deep repose is the sign
That you have reached the appointed goal

To return to the source is to discover
The eternal law of seed

He who returns to this eternal law is enlightened
Being enlightened he is serene
Serene he is open-hearted
Open-hearted he is beyond social games
Being beyond social games he is in tune with seed
In tune with see he endures

Until the end of his life he is not in peril

From *Psychedelic Prayers & Other Meditations*, Timothy Leary, Ronin, 1997.

by permission

18

DANGERS
OF PSYCHEDELICS

Are there any dangers involved with the use of psychedelics? Yes, there are. They are very powerful sacraments, or medicine, and they have to be approached with the utmost respect, preferably under the guidance of an experienced friend. The fears most commonly voiced are damage to body and brain as well as dangerous behavior and addiction. The classic psychedelics, unlike substances such as heroin, cocaine, and alcohol, have virtually no organic toxicity in the quantities in which they are ingested. Their addictive risk is too small to be measured when used in ceremonial settings. Psychedelic traditions from the Vedic dawn to Eleusis to the Native American Church have succeeded in creating ritual contexts in which hazardous acting-out is virtually unknown.

Psychedelics can trigger dramatic changes in the psyche and spirit, the heart/mind, in consciousness. Of course this effect is the very reason for taking them in the first place. Is it ultimately helpful or harmful?

Buddha recommends to view our life "as a dream, a flash in the darkness, a star in the morning dawn, a bubble in a stream, an illusion of the senses". The aim of practice is to wake up from that dream. One question often asked after a deep experience is: Was it a genuine awakening, or was it just another dream within a dream, another illusion within an illusion?

A primary religious experience is the seed for a spiritual life. No matter how genuine the encounter with the Ultimate might be, it does not guarantee a genuine spiritual life. The experience may be authentic, but what counts is our daily life. Will we be able to muster up the necessary determination and patience to let the light that we glimpsed for a moment, be it through meditation or psychedelics, gradually penetrate our whole being? Will we allow the experience of oneness and belonging - whether or not it wasn't really real - to inspire and transform our lives? This is our challenge and our hope, individually and as a species.

Bad Trips

The most common of all the negative aspects of psychedelics is the "bad trip", which is an exaggerated frightening experience that feels very real.

Bad trips are usually a result of poor planning. Bad trips can be avoided by paying attention to set and setting. The set is what you bring to the trip. Your mind. All your memories, your life experiences, how you are feeling at the moment of ingestion, your expectations of the trip, cur-

A bad trip is an exaggerated frightening experience that feels very real.

rent state of mind and so on.. It is best to be in a happy, relaxed mood with no immediate responsibilities that you will have to take care of for the next several hours. A bad trip is almost guaranteed if you trip right after a tragedy or saddening event in your life, as it is likely to make the problem worse. Unlike drinking or smoking weed, where you do it to get away from your problems, psychedelics make you face your problems head on, which may be a bad trip. Discovering a problem in your life and being enlightened on as how to fix it while on a psychedelic is an incredible feeling. But it takes patience, dedication, and mental strength. If you're just looking for a good time to relax and get away from your daily problems for a while, stick to weed. Psychedelics are not for you.

Setting

The setting is the physical environment where you trip. The best place is in a comfortable, familiar place where you may have some good memories. Music is also important. Relaxing, joyful music that you feel you may have a connection with is the best, and will help to calm you down if you feel like you're starting to have a bad trip.

The social setting is important. Are you tripping alone or with friends? Tripping alone is better for the more spiritual experience that psychedelics have to offer. But you should only trip alone if you are experienced. Someone that is inexperienced with this state of mind could end up in in a bad trip.

Tripping with friends is usually a good decision. Should something goe wrong, you'll have someone there to reassure you and spin your trip back to the right direction. Make sure however that these friends are people who you trust and who a sense of balance and maturity.

The number one cause of bad trips is forgetting that psychedelics are a temporary experience. They get to thinking that they have gone insane forever. It can help to write down the time you "dropped" and the does. Later reading this can be reassuring that it will all be over in a matter of hours and that there is no reason to panic.

If you do have a bad trip, do not go to a hospital. There is really nothing they can do to help you, it'll just make your trip worse by forcing you to sit around in a hospital bed for hours waiting for your trip to end.

Turning Around a Bad Trip

There are three tools for turning around a bad trip. Reassure the tripper that it will all be over soon. Remind him that is only on a drug, and that there is no reason to panic. Remind him to mellow out and go with the flow.

Another tool is to change the setting, specifically the location. Scary looking or unfamiliar settings could trigger bad trips.

Changing the music is a powerful way to mellow out a bad trip. Turn on something nice and joyful and mellow to listen to. Music has a powerful ability to change emotion.

The key is to avoid bad emotions. Thinking about confusion, loss, sadness, and other "downer" things, will ignite a downward spiral into a bad trip. Stay optimistic. Don't let these emotions take over you.

The more serious side of bad trips is on really high doses. Someone who experiences an incredibly traumatizing bad trip while on a very high dose of psychedelics could end up feeling somewhat depressed for a couple weeks, perhaps even months, though the feeling will pass with time. It is important to use psychedelic responsibility.

Mental Illnesses

While psychedelic drugs themselves have not been proven to cause any sort of mental illness, but they can bring out strong feelings that may be hidden to reveal itself in a person to its fullest extent, or to advance the progression of a disorder. For this reason, anyone with a strong family history of mental illness, or anyone who is showing strong symptoms of certain psychological disorders should absolutely avoid using psychedelics.

There is evidence that extremely frequent, heavy use of LSD (1-2 times a week for several months) can create a sort of mental disorder, or moreso, a feeling of being very detached from reality.

Use

Moderation is key. Caution suggests 2-4 months between each psychedelic experience. Take what you learn from your trip, apply it to your life, and then when you are ready to learn more, trip again.

Tolerance builds up quickly. Unlike marijuana and alcohol, where drinking/smoking regularly for a long period of time is needed to create a decent tolerance, tolerance to psychedelic can build up in just one trip. If you eat 2 grams of shrooms one day without any tolerance and you get a powerful trip, you would probably have to eat twice as much the next day to get the same high.

On the other hand, the tolerance drops a lot quicker than other drugs as well. It usually takes no more than one month to lose absolutely all of your tolerance. In fact, you probably lose something like 90% of that tolerance you built up in about 2 or 3 weeks.

Flashbacks

Another feared negative effect from psychedelics are "flashbacks". Flashbacks are a feeling like you are high on psychedelic without having actually taken any recently. Flashbacks can be both bad and good—they can come from a trau-matizing trip, or from an incredible trip. So flashbacks aren't necessarily always a bad thing

Flashbacks are a feeling like you are high on psychedelic without having actually taken any recently.

Flashbacks are usually short lived—a few minutes at most, and become less frequent as time passes by. It is generally accepted that flashbacks are caused when a person is reminded of a certain significant point in a trip they had, and it comes back to them as a very powerful memory of an incredibly emotional point in your life.

Flashbacks tend to occur more commonly with those who use psychedelics heavily. Most people never experi-ence them

HPPD

The final and perhaps most uncommon side effect of using psychedelics is something known as Hallucinogen Persisting Perception Disorder or HPPD. HPPD is essentially when once a trip ends, the visuals don't go away. For several weeks, perhaps months, and in the most rarest of cases, even years, a person may consistently experience psychedelic visuals.

It is generally believed by scientists that HPPD is linked to mental disturbances. Those more prone to mental illnesses are more likely to experience HPPD. HPPD is only known to build up in people who abuse psychedelics very heavily. Avoiding all drugs for as long as necessary will help make the disorder disappear, and it is accepted that HPPD is only a temporary effect. HPPD rare and is more likely to appear in very heavy users.

Who Should Avoid Psychedelics

Here is a basic, quick list of people who should probably just avoid psychedelics as a whole:

- Those who are on medications or anti depressants
- Anyone with a very strong family history of mental illnesses
- Anyone who is not completely 100% confident in their choice to experiment with psychedelics
- Anyone with a weak sense of their personality, ego, and who they are

HE WHO KNOWS
THE CENTER ENDURES

Who knows the outside is clever
Who knows the center endures
Who masters others gains robot power
Who comes to the center has flowering strength

Faith of cobnsciousness is freedom
Hope of consciousness is strength
Love of consciousness evokes the same in return

Faith of seed frees
Hope of seed flowers
Love of seed grows

From *Psychedelic Prayers & Other Meditations*, Timothy Leary, Ronin, 1997.
by permission

PART III

THE CHURCH OF THE AWAKENING

19

A FELLOWSHIP

The Church of the Awakening is a fellowship of those who ted to conscious participation in their own spiritual evolution and who are aware of the importance of the proper use of psychedelic plants or chemicals as a factor in that growth. We believe that the real purpose of life is growth in awareness, or the unfolding, the actualizing, of our inner spiritual potential. The word "spiritual" is used in this discussion to refer to that non-material reality that underlies material reality; the depths of our being, as distinguished from the surface manifestation; the awareness of ourselves as Being, or Life, rather than as the body or the personality in which that life is expressing itself.

In the process of spiritual growth, many techniques have been used, such as prayer, fasting, study of scriptures, meditation, mantras, surrender to a Higher Power, and service to others. As far back in history as we can probe, the ingestion of various plants, such as the peyote cactus in America, certain mushrooms in many areas, and soma in India, has also been a means of promoting growth in awareness, called by some "Self-realization."

Psychedelic Church

The Church of the Awakening, then, is not a psychedelic church in the sense that its only or even its chief function is to promote the use of psychedelic chemicals. It is, however, a psychedelic church in the wider meaning of the word "psychedelic," which is "mind-manifesting" or "consciousness-expanding."

The Church originated in a group that has been meeting in Socorro, New Mexico, since 1958 for study and discussion, exploring ways in which life might be made more meaningful.

My wife Louisa and I, both osteopathic physicians engaged in general medical practice since 1937, moved to Socorro in 1948. We continued practice there, she majoring in obstetrics, until our retirement in 1964. We were active members of the Presbyterian Church and participated in community affairs. I served one term as president of the Rotary Club and ten years as a member of the City Council.

Jolted

In 1951 we were severely jolted by the death by drowning of our younger son, David, in the crash of a U. S. Navy plane in the Mediterranean Sea. In 1957 our older son, Don, also a physician, drowned in a sailboat accident in Lake Huron. These events stimulated us to engage seriously in the search for the meaning of life. The answers provided by our church failed to satisfy us. for an admonition to intellectual belief could not meet a deep emotional need.

We found a few other people who had similar interests and needs, and the first meeting of the group was held on

October 12, 1958, with six persons attending. Meetings were held weekly, and attendance grew to thirty. The basic interest was in the exploration of man's potential. Many questions were asked with deep sincerity, and we experienced the truth of Jesus' statement, "Seek, and you will find."

Do We Live Again

Because of our personal bereavement, we began with the question of death. We were acutely aware of Job's yearning when he wrote, "Man that is born of woman is of few days and full of trouble. He comes forth like a flower, and withers. . . Man breathes his last, and where is he? If a man die, shall he live again?" This question is in the back of everyone's mind, but it had suddenly become the most important question in our lives, with immediate and personal urgency. The answers we found through our study and experience assure us that, if a man dies, he does live again (Ford and Bro, 1958) . It is more accurate, however, to say that death is not an ending, but only a continuation of life, with expression in a different form.

Our experiences led to further questions: Is consciousness confined to this physical body and its very limited senses? Are there other, "extra" senses? We know that a dog can hear sounds pitched too high for the human ear, and I know that many people can hear sounds that are inaudible to me. May it not be that there are some who are sensitive to entirely different types of frequencies that are unrecognized by most of us, and who may have "extrasensory perception" (ESP)?

The British and the American Societies for Psychical Research have accumulated much evidence that indicates that ESP is a fact that must be taken into consideration if we are to have a truer view of life. With this ESP, some can become aware of events taking place at a distance in space (clairvoyance). Some can become aware of events that will occur in the future (precognition). Some even seem able to communicate with the so-called dead (mediumship). Russian researchers have referred to persons with this extrasensory capacity as "biological radios," for they are able to "tune in" to these frequencies, unsensed by most of us, and to convert them to a type of stimulus to which we can respond. In this way, through one of these "biological radios," a man named Arthur Ford, we first received evidence that our sons were dead only in the physical sense. We found that they are still very much alive as personalities, functioning in a different way. This seemed to be evidence that the world of the physical senses is only the surface of a reality that is actually much more vast.

Is consciousness confined to this physical body and its very limited senses?

We next became intrigued by reports of seemingly miraculous healing, which resulted when certain individuals or groups prayed for, or in some cases placed their hands on, the sick. (We should recognize that so-called miracles are only the manifestation of laws we do not as yet understand.)

We read reports by Rebecca Beard, M.D. (1950) of a personal healing and of other cases she observed, indicating that there is a healing force beyond that produced by medications, or even by the co-operation of the subconscious mind of the patient. Dr. Alexis Carrel witnessed

almost unbelievable healings at Lourdes, in France (1950).
Ambrose and Olga Worrall, of Baltimore, are two among
many who seem to be channels for this healing power today (1965). Other strange manifestations of this power are
reported by Harold Sherman after careful and extensive
observation of "wonder" healers in the Philippines (1967).

In our own experience, one evening as we were praying
for healing, and focusing our love on various people present, I felt impelled to put my hands on a woman present,
named Natalie, who had a serious heart ailment. As I
placed my hands on her, my left on the upper chest, the
right on the upper back, I felt a surge of power, much like
a strong electrical current, flowing through my right arm
and hand. There remained a sensation of numbness in the
arm and hand for some fifteen minutes afterward.

I had X-rayed Natalie previously and found her heart
enlarged to almost twice normal size. Upon re-X-ray a
month later, the heart size was normal, and her symptoms
greatly improved. What happened, or whether this incident had anything to do with the healing, I do not know.
I do know that something unusual happened, and that
many others have had more-striking experiences of a similar nature. In the New Testament, James says, "The prayer
of faith will save the sick man, and the Lord will raise him
up." We studied, we experimented, as many others are
doing, and we found that it is so.

20

FACE TO FACE
WITH LIFE

It seemed that we had no choice but to continue to explore the depths of the mind and of consciousness. As we did so, we found ourselves coming face to face with life itself. We began to be dimly aware that our own true nature is this depth, which is life, or consciousness, and which is universal, omnipotent, and omnipresent. Many call it God. To discover that this is what we really are, rather than the body, the mind, or the personality, involves a radical shift in perspective. There are many who fear to experience this shift.

Many of the questions we were asking, and the areas of our explorations, seem to be off limits in most religious and scientific circles. Those who begin such "metaphysical" (beyond the physical) seeking are likely to become suspect by their friends who have chosen to accept the teachings of orthodoxy, whether scientific or religious. New ideas are regarded by many as threats to the ego, to personal security. Perhaps this is a part of the instinct for self-preservation, which we all have. When our mental structure of ideas is threatened, we become as defensive as when the physical body is in danger, for much effort has been invested in each case.

Dangerous Enterprise

There were many in Socorro who felt that the members of our group were engaged in a very dangerous enterprise, and many warnings were given that we should return to the fold. The minister of one local church, several of whose members were attending our meetings, warned that such groups could be useful, but that a minister (presumably of his particular denomination!) should always be present to be sure that we did not go too far afield. The minister of another church, when invited to discuss with our group what his religion meant to him, declined the invitation. He said that the explorations in which we were engaged were not approved by the community, and he did not care to risk his reputation by meeting with us. A patient told one of our group that the Aikens had seemed to be fine people, and good doctors, but now that they had developed such strange ideas, they could no longer be trusted.

This, of course, was a threat to our security! Some of the members of the group could not stand the pressure of this negative public opinion, and withdrew. The majority remained, and we continued to inquire into the nature and purpose of life. One finds a great challenge in this quest, and a very deep inner satisfaction in the results. When one has experienced reality, there is little interest in mere beliefs about reality. 'When one has seen the ocean, he no longer has any need to "believe in" its existence. It is almost impossible to return to any orthodox teachings that seem inconsistent with one's own personal experience. We could only continue on the path we had chosen, even in the face of public disapproval.

ESP and Parapsychology

At first, as has been said, we investigated the phenomena of ESP and the findings of parapsychology. As the interests of the group expanded, we became aware of the writings and experiences of the mystics of the world, including such people as Meister Eckhart, Thomas Kelly, Evelyn Underhill, Ramana Maharshi, Huang Po, the Hindu rishis, and the Sufis. They were of various cultures and religions. They seemed to have explored the deepest mysteries of life and experienced reality in depth. Many of the things that they have to say seem very strange from an intellectual point of view but strike a note of deep understanding from the perspective of experience. From this perspective also, the life and teachings of Jesus took on more-challenging and more-vital significance. For the little group in Socorro, the search was becoming more and more rewarding.

In 1959 we had our first information on the psychedelic substances, through reading an article in a scientific journal by Dr. Humphry Osmond, then medical director of the Saskatchewan Provincial Hospital, in Canada (1957). Dr. Osmond reported on research dealing with the effects produced by the ingestion of such substances as LSD, mescaline, and peyote. He pointed out that new depths of awareness seemed to develop during this drug-induced state, and in this article proposed the word "psychedelic" for these substances, as being more accurate than the word "hallucinogenic," which was then in common use.

More important than the state of awareness that many developed, it seemed that insights attained during this experience could be applied to the problems of everyday life and their solution. Most interesting to us was Dr. Osmond's observation that the psychedelic state seemed often to be very similar to the mystical state, in the study of which we were at that time engaged.

Correspondence with Dr. Osmond brought additional information and the names of others who were doing research with these psychedelic substances. All were most helpful in sharing with us the results of their work and advising us as to the best ways in which to proceed with our own investigations. At that time we found that we could obtain peyote, a cactus that grows in the southern Rio Grande Valley. It seemed effective in inducing, in much greater depth, a type of awareness or mystical experience that some of us had already experienced, to a lesser degree, as a result of using other spiritual disciplines.

Mystical Experience

By "mystical experience" is meant here a state of consciousness in which the individual finds a oneness with the universe, and feels unconditional love for God, his neighbor, and himself. All are realized as One. It is not unlike the state of one who is deeply in love. In Eastern terminology this is called Self-realization, liberation, enlightenment, or satori. The Christian may call it a vital experience of God, or coming to know Christ. The psychologist may call it the creative integration of the personality around a deep center. By whatever name it may be called, it seems to those who have experienced it to be the way toward the actualization of our ultimate potential as human beings,

toward the identification as that Life, or Divinity, which is
the reality of each living being.

In the early days of our exploration of these deeper
levels of consciousness, one of our group experienced a
very marked change in his outlook as a result of the peyote
sacrament. Prior to this he had been an atheist, but after
his participation in the sacrament he said, "I have experienced God! I know that reality is there, that it is desirable
above all things, and that it is attainable. Now I am willing
to take the path of effort, to earn the right to have and to
keep this reality. I know that I, too, may become the way,
the truth, and the life."

21

PEYOTE OPENED THE DOOR

To many it seems strange that the ingestion of a cactus can change one's outlook on life so dramatically, but modem chemistry has produced many compounds that modify the mind of man by changing the chemistry of the body. Tranquilizers—chemicals that relieve tensions, neuroses, and even psychoses—are well known. The psychedelics, however, when properly used, have a more constructive effect in that they may help produce understanding, and thus, unlike the tranquilizers, can remove the cause of the tensions, occasionally in a single dose. They have the unusual effect of opening wider the doors of perception and self-understanding. On the physical level, they enable one to see with new vision and to hear with new appreciation. A great many who have been through this experience find a much keener enjoyment of nature, of flowers, trees, mountains, and a greater appreciation of the arts. On an extended level, one may develop an awareness of an all-inclusive spiritual reality, which, the masters have told us, is the substance, the Ground of Being, that underlies the world of both the senses and the "extra-senses."

Our explorations with peyote went on, and we were more and more impressed with the importance of the effects of this substance when taken by people with a motivation toward better understanding of themselves and of life, and when given by one with similar motivation and an awareness of the hazards of improper use. Later we experimented with the use of mescaline, the psychedelic alkaloid present in the peyote cactus, and found the effects to be identical with those we had obtained through the use of peyote itself.

> *Our explorations with peyote went on, and we were more and more impressed with the importance of the effects of this substance.*

We were not alone in our explorations, and soon found others with similar interests in the religious use of these substances. In 1962 and 1963 the public was beginning to develop a very negative image of the psychedelics, especially LSD, as a result of sensationalism in the news media when reporting some of the unfortunate results of their unsupervised use. We were disturbed by the possibility that indiscriminate use for sensational purposes was likely to bring about restrictive legislation that would interfere with their use for religious purposes. My wife and I made two trips to Los Angeles to discuss this matter with interested friends there, and it was suggested that our group should incorporate as a non-profit organization or church, in which the use of psychedelics as a religious sacrament might be legally continued.

Founding of the Church

The idea seemed to have merit, and continued to develop. On October 14, 1963, the Church of the Awakening was incorporated under the laws of the state of New Mexico as a non-profit religious organization. The psychedelic experience was named as a sacrament of the Church, to be available only to those who have been members of the Church for a minimum period of three months, and whose readiness for the sacrament is approved by the Board of Directors. It is recommended that the experience not be repeated more frequently than every three months, for it seems to us that frequent use of these substances is likely to result for some in a desire for the experience for its own sake, rather than in the more important application of insights achieved to the development of a better way of life.

Our limitations on the use of the sacrament were also imposed in order to avoid some of the unfortunate results that were being reported in the news media from frequent and unsupervised use of large amounts of LSD by those who had little idea of what might result. When one takes a psychedelic "for kicks" and suddenly finds himself confronting what seems like Ultimate Reality, it is then too late to retreat, and panic frequently develops. It seems to us highly important to protect the proper religious use, and also to protect novices from unnecessary hazards.

Our goal has been to attract members who are interested primarily in spiritual growth and who are willing to follow the usual disciplines and practices for such growth both as a preparation for the sacrament and as a continuing follow-up. We are well aware of the importance of other methods of Self-realization. We have found, however, that the psychedelic sacrament, when added to the spiritual armamentarium, can be of great value in the search for meaning.

Religious Sacrament

In our use of the experience as a religious sacrament with many people, we have seen some unpleasant, but no harmful, effects. Many seem to be outstandingly constructive. The experience of the atheist who found God seemed to us to be constructive. Another, who had little or no appreciation of music, now delights in his collection of classical records. Another found a new understanding and acceptance of her husband. Another has been able to relate more lovingly to her Children, We are always pleased with the attitude that many express after their participation in the sacrament by saying, I have seen so many things in myself that need changing that I am sure I will not want another experience for at least a Year!

Other experimenters, using these substances in ways somewhat similar to ours, have reported similar results. The work in progress at the Spring Grove Hospital since 1963 on the treatment of alcoholism indicates that many alcoholics, when they attain this degree of self-understanding, are able to recover from alcoholism, sometimes after only a single experience. This is in accord with the statement of Bill Wilson, the founder of Alcoholics Anonymous, that the most important factor in recovery from the disease of alcoholism is ". . . a deep and genuine religious experience." We have found that, for many, a properly oriented psychedelic experience can be a deep and genuine religious experience.

Personal Experience

Religious or spiritual experience, like any other, is intensely personal and cannot be conveyed in words to one who has not had something similar. We cannot convey even the taste of a strange fruit to one who has not tasted it. The closest we can come to it is to say that it is "something like" the taste of another which we have both experienced. Again, how could we describe the color red, or any color, or even the sense of vision, to one who was born blind?

When one explores this inner space, the depths of consciousness (Jesus called it "the Kingdom of Heaven which is Within you"), he finds experiences that have no counterpart in ordinary life, and so is at a loss as to how he can explain it to one who has not explored. All that he can say is, You must experience it for yourself before you will really understand.

Rights Denied

There seems to be no way in which legislators, or the general public to whom they are sensitive, can be made directly aware of the religious benefits of a properly directed psychedelic sacrament except through having the experience. There is still, however, some degree of respect, both among legislators and the general public, for religious sacraments, even those that may seem rather strange to some. The right of the Indians of the Native American Church to continue the use of peyote as a sacrament, as it has been used for hundreds of years, has been recognized by governmental agencies, in spite of all efforts of fanatics to deny them this right. The Code of Federal Regulations states, in Section 166.3 (c) (3) of Title 1, "The listing of peyote in this sub-paragraph (as being restricted or forbidden) does not apply to non-drug use in bona fide religious ceremonies of the Native American Church." We feel that other races should have equal rights before the law and that the Church of the Awakening should be able to continue its use of peyote as a religious sacrament. While the use of peyote or other psychedelics is not our primary purpose, we have found it to be a highly important aid to spiritual growth or "awakening." No one of the sacraments of the Christian churches is the primary purpose of any church, but each is an important aid to spiritual growth.

Naming the Church

The name Church of the Awakening was selected after careful consideration of our orientation and motivation. The explorations in awareness, of "inner space," such as those we have described, result for many in a new perspective. It is a new state of consciousness, in which all things are perceived as One. This state cannot be comprehended intellectually, but it can be experienced by those who are ready for it. Readiness seems usually, though not always, to be a result of serious dedication to the inner quest.

'When one has achieved this new perspective, his former state seems like a dream by comparison, in which he was unaware of many of the facets and relationships of life. David, in Psalm 17, says, "When I awake, I shall be satisfied with beholding Thy form." When Gautama Siddhartha, some twenty-five hundred years ago, achieved this mystical insight, he was asked what it was that made him view life so differently. He replied, "I am awake!" In his language, the word was "buddha," and so he came to be called "The Buddha," or "The One Who Is Awake." The Church of the Awakening is intended to be a fellowship of those who are seeking for this experience in depth, for this awakening.

Our purpose is not to present a body of doctrine for the acceptance of members, nor to furnish ultimate intellectual answers to the basic questions of life. The purpose of this fellowship is to encourage growth and awakening on the part of each member, to stimulate him to ask questions, to develop insights, and to encourage the sharing with others of such insights as a loving service.

22

BELIEF & DOUBT

Belief is a first stage in the religious life, but when we are ready to question, then we can begin to grow into the more mature stage of experience. Is this not true also in science? The student believes what his books and teachers tell him, but he is expected to prove it for himself in the laboratory, and in life. True doubt, then, is a constructive force, for when we question earnestly, we begin to experiment, and experiment leads to experience. We know then, from deep within ourselves, because of our own experience, what we formerly only believed because someone else had said that it was so. Our use of the psychedelic sacrament is an important factor in growth from the stage of belief to that of experience of spiritual truths.

The Church of the Awakening, therefore, encourages doubt, questioning, and experiment as the way of growth, the way of life.

The Church of the Awakening, therefore, encourages doubt, questioning, and experiment as the way of growth, the way of life. This process must begin at a different point for each individual. Each one is unique; each is the result of past causes —thoughts, feelings, and actions. Each is encouraged to participate in his own growth, to promote his own spiritual evolution, to be, as St. Paul says, ". . . a cocreator with God." We feel that such growth, such evolution, is the true purpose of all religion. In fact, such growth is religion!

Like any other tool, the intellect is very useful for some purposes, but of little or no value for others.

Each of us must begin and continue the long, difficult— and joyous!—process of living life. There must be willingness to fail if there is to be any chance of success. There must be acceptance of ourselves and of others, with all our present defects and limitations. These defects and limitations are but the promise that growth and evolution can take place.

Growth of Inner Life

The Church of the Awakening is dedicated to this ideal of enhancing the growth of the inner life of each member, and also the expression of that growth through more-enlightened service. We note that the greatest service does not always consist in removing the problems of another, but more often in encouraging him to meet those problems as opportunities for growth.

Inner growth, or learning, and outer service, or sharing, can be encouraged in the traditional ways, but should be without the traditional bondage to forms and rituals. Forms and rituals may be used when desired, but should not become an end in themselves. Every means to the end of growth should itself be outgrown. When the growth has been achieved, the means should be discarded, as is the scaffolding used to erect a building. One may use a raft to cross a stream, but he is handicapped if he tries to carry it on his shoulders as he explores the other shore.

In addition to such traditional forms and rituals as may be used, which should change with the changing needs and desires of the group, we encourage the study of the writings of sages and mystics. We need to become acquainted with the lives and perspectives of those of past and present generations who have attained at least some measure of freedom from selfishness and egotism, which both the Christ and the Buddha pointed out were the cause of all our difficulties.

Another very important and useful means for sharing insights and for mutual help in the process of growth is the meeting of members and friends at stated times. In this group activity, two practices are helpful. One is sharing through discussion. The other is sharing through silence. By means of discussion, the sharing of ideas, we become able to change our old ways of thinking, to adapt to new ideas, to develop the intellectual aspect of life.

Meditation

Sharing through silence, or meditation, however, is likely to be a greater stimulus to spiritual growth and the development of understanding. How can silence be so important in spiritual growth? We are usually led to believe that a powerful intellect, with a large supply of self-consistent concepts, is the supreme human achievement. We have even been taught that we are the intellect. But when one has been privileged to have a mystical experience, whether spontaneous, the result of spiritual disciplines, or induced by means of psychedelic substances, he experiences a Self of which the intellect is only a tool.

Like any other tool, the intellect is very useful for some purposes, but of little or no value for others. If we are to achieve this glimpse of the depths of awareness, or the "Awakening," the intellect must be quieted in order that we may go beyond it, to That which is its source.

Words are symbols of ideas, of concepts. Concepts, in turn, are symbols that point to an experience. When our attention is focused on words, or on concepts, we fail to achieve the depths of the experience they represent. Meditation or silence (inner as well as outer) is practice in going beyond concepts to the Self, which is the reality underlying all thoughts, feelings, and actions. "Be still, and know," the Psalmist says.

23

PATH OF INNER EXPLORATION

As one follows the path of inner exploration, it may happen that psychic powers develop. These powers include such abilities as clairvoyance, telepathy, precognition, healing, or communication with the after-death level of life. Such powers may, if properly used, be a help in turning our awareness from the outer to the inner life; "biological radio," as discussed earlier, was very helpful to me at one stage. However, if sought as ends in themselves, psychic powers can be a hindrance in our quest for That which is beyond all phenomena, whether physical, mental, or psychic. It is well, for example, that one should have a strong, properly functioning physical body; but to become an Atlas, to make physical strength an end in itself, is to be caught again in the trap of the ego. Psychic powers may be useful, just as physical strength is useful; but both are means rather than ends in themselves. The primary purpose of the Church of the Awakening has been stated to be the enhancement of growth in love and understanding, and the concurrent diminution of egotism and selfishness.

Our purpose may also be furthered by individual and group participation in the psychedelic sacrament or mystical initiation. We believe that this sacrament should be administered only to those who have prepared and qualified themselves for it, and only by properly trained monitors or ministers of the Church. Such administration should be in accord with the laws of the United States, and also of the state in which a particular Church group is located. If such laws seem restrictive of reasonable religious freedom, then when the time is appropriate the members may seek for an improvement in the legal situation.

Insight

In the life of the spirit, the psychedelic sacrament is also considered to be a means to growth, and not an end in itself. Of more importance is the development of insight, which results from participation in this experience, and the intelligent application of this insight in service to our fellow men and the improvement of our own character. It seems that we do have a choice as to

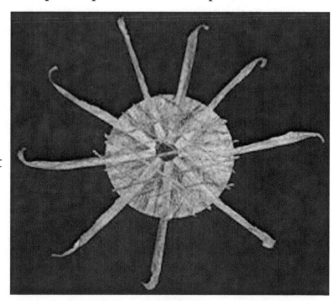

whether we integrate or disintegrate, and that the investment of conscious effort toward integration is necessary and important in the development of character. Our goal for members of the Church is true integration, or Unitary Consciousness, which to us is the actualization through growth, aided by effort, of the highest potential inherent within each one.

We hope to develop ministers to serve the Church whose philosophy of life is in harmony with this outlook and who are also capable of administering the psychedelic sacrament. There are excellent monitors within the "psychedelic cult," but many are likely to regard the psychedelic experience as an end in itself, while others are careless of the legal situation. Among professional researchers in the psychedelic field, some do not have the religious or spiritual orientation we have attempted to express. Others, who may have this orientation, may not care to have their positions jeopardized by making it public. Our culture is heavily materialistic and is likely to reject any who attempt to follow another path. We are seeking men and women who can and will dedicate themselves to this type of growth and service.

Self-Realization

We have emphasized the importance of the mystical experience as a means of spiritual growth, but whether it results from the psychedelic sacrament or from the practice of other spiritual disciplines, it is only the beginning, and not the end, on

> *The psychedelic sacrament is only the beginning, and not the end, on the path to Self-realization.*

the path to Self-realization. It is evident that we should evolve beyond isolated moments of perception, or insight, or mystical experience. Our real growth consists in fusing such moments into the continuum of life. No doubt this is what St. Paul had in mind when he wrote, "Rejoice always, pray without ceasing, be grateful in all circumstances."

We would avoid, in the Church of the Awakening, the temptation to rely on the momentary experience and the desire to seek to repeat it frequently. We would encourage the application of insights and the development of new patterns of thought, feeling, and action more nearly in line with That which we have seen is our real Self.

Irving Babbitt, in his introduction to The Dhammapada (1936), comments that the readiness of men to succumb to schemes for acquiring sudden wealth is perhaps only a faint image of their proneness to yield to the lure of teachings that seem to hold out the hope of spiritual riches without any corresponding effort. Especially in America, he says, substantial material reward awaits any one who can devise some new and painless plan for getting "in tune with the Infinite."

There are many who are still hopeful that the use of LSD will prove to be such a painless plan; that it will save us, if not from our sins, at least from spiritual effort. Men seek to enjoy the fruits of renunciation, although renouncing nothing. They seek to achieve the ends, but to avoid the means, which seem difficult and arduous. The glimpse of reality achieved by psychedelic means or in other ways is only that—a glimpse. We have seen the mountain, and know the direction in which we must go. Repeatedly gazing at the mountain does not satisfy the mountaineer.

He must place his own feet upon the path and climb it for himself. In fact, the greatest joy is found in the challenge of the climb. As one of our members, quoted earlier, said, "I have experienced God! Now I am willing to take the path of effort." So often we overlook the fact that one of the great satisfactions in life is found in overcoming, in meeting challenges. It is said in the Hindu scriptures that he who overcomes himself is greater than he who overcomes a multitude of the enemy. In the Christian scriptures, it is said, "He who overcomes shall have the fountain of the waters of Life."

Maturity teaches us that the reward is in the climbing, rather than in the arriving. The joy of life comes in living. Dr. Bernard Phillips, of Temple University, titled one of his lectures "The Search will make you free" (1964). Jesus said, "Seek, and you will find." When we find the seeking, the search, we are free!!

It would seem that the state of expanded awareness and insight frequently achieved during the psychedelic state can be validated only by further effort in the following of spiritual disciplines in re-creating character. Mystical insight can make us aware of our own egocentricity and selfishness, and can challenge us to engage in the process of overcoming, of self-transformation and self-transcendence. It can challenge us to fulfill ourselves by "dying"; then, as St. Paul expressed it, "It is no longer I, but Christ that lives." A seed must give up its life as a seed, in order that it might become a channel for life.

The Church of the Awakening seeks to encourage this development of the inner life, not through imposing an authoritative teaching, but through voluntary choice and individual effort on the part of each member. We are learning that there are no recipes for life. Love is the law, of course, but each must choose how he will apply it, each instant. We cannot accept old doctrines that divide rather than unite, nor old shibboleths of nationalism when they demand unloving acts; nor can we unthinkingly accept old codes of conduct that we see have brought our world to the brink of chaos. Before rejecting the old, however, we must have sufficient spiritual maturity to choose new directions that will be in closer harmony with life.

The Church of the Awakening is not unique in facing these situations, and we also recognize that all problems, of whatever nature, are opportunities for learning, for growth, and for actualizing our potential. We know that a tree that is subjected to the buffeting of wind and weather can develop great strength in depth. We know also that it is life that is living us, that it is life that is doing all things that are done. We know that life holds the final answers. Each of us has only to do, to the best of his ability, that which is before him, and life will arrange all things well.

As we engage in these challenges of the outer world, we must not allow ourselves to be distracted from the inner quest, or we will have lost the way. We need to maintain our awareness of the inexhaustible mystery of life. We find it helpful to encourage this awareness in various ways:

through association with mature people, through exposure to great literature, through the practice of meditation, and by means of the psychedelic sacrament.

Wordsworth, in Tintern Abbey, gives us the spirit of the inner life, on which a harmonious outer life can be built:

> *I have felt*
>
> *A presence that disturbs me with the joy Of elevated thoughts; a sense sublime*
>
> *Of something far more deeply interfused. Whose dwelling is the light of setting suns,*
>
> *And the round ocean and the living air, And the blue sky, and in the mind of man: A motion and a spirit, that impels*
>
> *All thinking things, all objects of thought, And rolls through all things.*

PART IV
TECHNIQUES

24

BREATHE SLOWLY

Breathing is the bridge between the body and the mind. By regulating breathing, you regulate your mind and emotions. When you breathe rapidly and shallowly you rile up the body; whereas when you breathe slowly and deeply your body and mind relax. Most adults tend to breathe shallowly by moving the upper chest, while deep breathing is facilitated by moving the belly. Diaphragmatic breathing is best for meditation. It better oxygenates the blood and calms the mind.

Check How You breathe

You probably haven't spent much time thinking about how yo breathe. You just breathe. There are different ways of breathing and each impacts the body and mind differently. You can check how you breath with the following simple exercise.

- Rest one hand on your upper chest and the other over your navel area.
- Breathe normally for a minute or so
- Notice which hand rises first when you inhale.

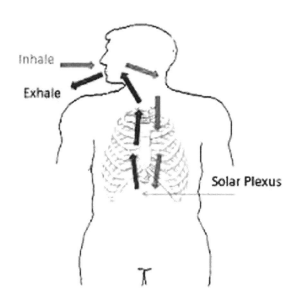

Inhale

Exhale

Solar Plexus

When the upper hand rises first you are using upper chest breathing. When the lower hand rises first you are breathing with your diaphragm. When both move at the same time you are using a mix of both.

Diaphragmatic breathing, also called abdominal breathing, belly breathing or deep breathing, is breathing that is done by contracting the diaphragm, a muscle located horizontally between the thoracic cavity and abdominal cavity. Air enters the lungs and the belly expands during this type of breathing. The diaphragm is the most efficient muscle of breathing. Your abdominal muscles help move the diaphragm and give you more power to empty your lungs. Diaphragmatic breathing is also the most natural and healthiest way of breathing. Observe how a very young baby breathes – they will use their diaphragm/belly with each breath.

Diaphragmatic breathing is a first step in normalizing your breathing to manage anxiety or feelings of panic as well as to facilitate deep meditation.

Diaphragmatic Breathing Technique

- Lie down on a flat surface like your bed or the floor or in bed Bend your need and support your head with a pillow. Some people use a pillow under their knees to support their legs. To feel your diaphragm as you breathe, place one hand on your upper chest and the other just below your rib cage.

- Breathe in slowly through your nose so that your stomach moves out against your hand. The hand on your chest should remain as still as possible.

- Tighten your stomach muscles and let them fall inward as you exhale through pursed lips. Keep the hand on your upper chest still.

- Many find it easier when first learning diaphragmatic breathing to follow the instructions while lying down. As you become skilled you can practice while sitting in a chair.

Use Your Diaphragm

Notice your breathing whenever you think of it. Spend a few minutes a couple of times a day practicing using your diaphragm:

- Sit in an upright position looking straight ahead. Close your eyes to concentrate on the process.

- Put one palm on your upper chest and the other over your navel. Your objective is to have the lower hand rise first when you breathe in.

- Breathe out gently and effortlessly. Wait for a second or two until the body spontaneously begins the inhalation, which will occur naturally and of its own accord.

- Allow the air to naturally flow in again until it stops, again of its own accord. Don't try to deepen the inhalation. Instead allow your body to find its natural rate of breathing. Then let your breathing to slow down.

- Continue doing breathing in this manner for 5 to 10 minutes.

The 4-7-8 Breathing Exercise

The 4-7-8 Breathing Exercise is a favorite of Andrew Weil, MD, which he recommends for relaxing. The exercise is simple, takes little time, requires no equipment and can be done anywhere. You can practice in any position. When learning the exercise, it helps to sit with your back straight back chair.

Place the tip of your tongue against the ridge of tissue just behind your upper front teeth, and keep it there through the entire exercise. Exhale through your mouth around your tongue.

- Exhale completely through your mouth, making a whoosh sound.

- Close your mouth and inhale quietly through your nose to a mental count of four.

- Hold your breath for a count of seven.

- Exhale completely through your mouth, making a whoosh sound to a count of eight.

- This is one breath. Now inhale again and repeat the cycle three more times for a total of four breaths.

Always inhale quietly through your nose and exhale audibly through your mouth, while keeping the tip of your tongue in position. The absolute time you spend on each phase is not important; the ratio of 4:7:8 is important. If you have trouble holding your breath, speed the exercise up but keep to the ratio of 4:7:8 for the three phases. With practice you can slow it all down and get used to inhaling and exhaling more and more deeply.

This exercise is subtle when you first try it and gains in power with repetition and practice. Do it at least twice a day. You cannot practice too frequently. Do no more than four breaths at one time for the first month of practice. Later, you can extend it to eight breaths. You may feel a little lightheaded when you first breathe this way; it will pass.

Breathing is a useful tool that you always have with you. Use it whenever anything upsetting happens—before you react. Use it whenever you are aware of internal tension. Use it to help you fall asleep. Use it to facilitate meditation.

25

DEVELOPS MIND SKILLS

There are four mind skills that meditation helps to develop: Focus, awareness, detachment and patience. Each of these skills are invaluable assets for negotiating daily life and handling difficulties.

Focus

Focus is the ability to stay concentrated on what you're doing and to ignore distractions. Focus is a central skill used during meditation. Meditation isn't clearing the mind as many think. It is focusing on one thing—usually one's breath. When the mind wanders, the meditation isn't a failure. The brain is like a young puppy—just a little out of control. Catching the mind when it wanders and bringing it back to the object of focus is the process of mediation. It's not a failure when your mind wanders—and it will. It's natural, especially when you're new to meditation.

The Mind is Like a Wild Elephant

The mind is like a wild elephant. If you put a chain on an elephant's leg and stake ti to the ground to contain it. The elephant will try to run away. When it does, you don't scold the elephant. Instead, take the chain and pull the elephant back. As soon as you do, the elephant will

run off again. Again, take the chain and pull the elephant back to focus. Again and again, the elephant will run off. Again and again, take the chain and pull the elephant back. By dong this, eventually the elephant will learn that you are the master.

Monkey Mind

Monkey mind is a Buddhist concept meaning "unsettled; restless; capricious; whimsical; fanciful; inconstant; con- fused; indecisive; uncontrollable". It refers to the busy chatter and distraction of thinking.

Buddha observed that just as a monkey swinging through the trees grabs one branch and lets it go only to seize another, so too, that which is called thought, mind or consciousness arises and disappears continually both day and night. Anyone who has spent even a little time observing one's mind and then watched a troop of mon- keys will see that this comparison is an accurate. Another time Buddha said that a person with uncontrolled craving jumps from here to there like a monkey searching for fruit in the forest.

Buddha instructed his disciples to train themselves so as to develop `a mind like a forest deer. Deer are particularly gentle creatures and always remain alert and aware no matter what they are doing.

Rebel Zen Master, Seamus Anthony, author of Psychedelic Meditation, says

> *"It is common to all humans that our mind actually rambles away at several different voices about different things all at once. To combat this, I developed a method of identifying a voice, by which I mean clearly identifying a little voice in my head rabbiting along about God knows-what, and then silencing it. Silencing it is not hard, but the identifying of all the voices can be, it is almost like they willfully try to speak as quietly as they can so that you won't notice. And every time I did identify and silence a voice, I would become aware of another, until I was fairly sure I had quietened them all down. But then I would realize that I was—on another level—talking to myself about finding little voices and extinguishing them!"*

"My mind races, I get the fidgets, I feel like packing it in and going back to be or doing something else, but the key is—if you wait this out then you set yourself up for an awesome and amazingly blissful experience. An experience as good as great sex, or a clean drug high, or that great feeling you get when you are doing something that

Your thoughts are like clouds floating across an eternally peaceful sky of awareness that is ever-present.

you love, of the adrenaline rush that sports-people get when playing sport or stage performers feel during and just after a great show. You can enjoy this feeling over and over again, and the flow on effects of this will spread into your day to day life—you'll be happier, light of heart and less stressed."

Meditation is not about stopping thoughts as commonly misunderstood. Rather it is your mind developing an impartial awareness of itself and its workings. By observing dispassionately, without judgment and criticism, you learn that your emotions are not you.

Rebel Zen Master goes on to say, "Your thoughts are not your mind but rather they are like clouds floating across an eternally peaceful sky of awareness that is ever-present." Focus is "the stake that we tether the Monkey Mind to so that it doesn't get out of control and start bossing us around."

Mind Focus Workout

1) Bring your focus to your breath.

2) Notice that your mind has wandered off.

3) Disengage from that train of thought.

4) Bring your focus back to your breath and hold it there.

The next time you notice your mind wandering off to wondering what your son is doing rather than your breath, for example, let the thought go and bring your attention back to your breath. You do this over and over during meditation. Meditation is a process of teaching your mind to focus. This seemingly simple mental routine is deceptive. It looks easier than it actually is. Try it for one minute, and if you're like most of us, you'll find your mind wanders off to some other thought.

It takes mindfulness—an active attention to notice that your mind has drifted, and a mental effort to end that reverie and go back to the breath. When you regularly practice mindfulness you will find it easier to keep your focus where you want it to be.

Awareness

When we raise our consciousness, we become more aware of the sensations in the body and we feel that the sensations change. An intense sensation that is pain and an intense sensation that is pleasure, both become pleasurable.

Focusing keeps your eyes on the road, but awareness lets you enjoy the scenery. Almost all the satisfaction of a sitting comes not from watching the road but from those sideways glances at the scenery.
The physiological shifts, the bodily tranquility, the pleasure of mental freedom are all part of the scenery. When you're focused, you only see the breath.

Focusing keeps your eyes on the road, but awareness lets you enjoy the scenery.

Since awareness is already part of every meditation, the instructions are unique to it. In an awareness meditation, you don't have any new object to focus on. It's more about shifting your emphasis when you meditate from focusing to watching, from spotlight consciousness to floodlight consciousness. You become a spectator—an observer.

In most meditations, you focus inwardly on the meditation object. When practicing awareness, you do the opposite. You still have a focal point, which could be anything at all, but most of your attention goes outward, "just watching" the passing thoughts and sensations.

When doing a formal breath meditation, for example, you would only notice other thoughts and sensations when they grab your attention. When practicing awareness, however, you may still be focusing on the breath, but you allow other thoughts to surface. You deliberately watch them as they pass through consciousness.

Keep the mind neutral. Aim for a bland, mirror-like mind. Don't think about what is happening. Don't chase good things or resist bad things; just notice what enters your mind.

Detachment

A noble truth tells us that the root of all suffering is attachment. To avoid suffering, we need to understand what causes suffering and then weed out these causes. According to Buddha, the basic cause of suffering is "the attachment to the desire to have (craving) and the desire not to have (aversion)".

We all have desires and cravings. Because we cannot satisfy all our desires and cravings, we get agitated and angry, which is a manifestation of suffering. Buddha also pointed out that denying desire—depriving oneself—is like denying life itself. A person has to rise above attachments and for that, he need not deprive himself. The problem arises when he does not know where to put an end to his desires. And when he yields in to his desires, he becomes a slave to them.

Patience

Maintaining patience during meditation is of vital importance. Showing signs of impatience is a sign that you need to meditate. Experiencing less impatience comes with regular meditation practice. The process usually looks something like this:

1. Before meditation we often experience impatience, but are not always aware of it and not always able to label it as impatience.

2. When we meditation, we tend to see things more clearly and may think we are experiencing more impatience. However, this is not the case, it is simply a matter of having more clarity and being able to identify it as impatience.

3. As we meditate on a regular basis, we tend to become more clear about our feelings, and those that trouble us tend to decrease as our resistance toward them lessens.

The most important aspect to remember throughout is that patience is not something we need to develop. Instead, we need to learn how to let go of impatience. This may sound like the same thing, but it's actually quite different.

Patience is an inherent part of a calm and clear mind. When we know this and understand it, then we do not try to "create" patience; instead we simply let go of the noise and our involvement in that activity and

When we feel that we need to try and "create" patience, then we will likely feel more stressed about the process, perhaps spend a lot of time thinking about the process, possibility and potential, and may even create more impatience in the mind.

26

ASSUME A BEGINNER'S MIND

Psychedelics can inspire the "beginner's mind' and get you out of the habits and ruts of your life that stand in the way of a fresh, direct experience. The dramatic rise of interest in Yoga, meditation and eastern religion in the 60s and 70s was closely related to the psychedelic movement.

During the 80s and 90s many of the spiritual, ex-hippie communities became middle-aged meditation centers with few members 30 years old. The next generation seemed less interested in meditation, alternative lifestyles or psychedelics. However, there now seems to be renewed interest among younger adults in with mind-altering plants and chemicals.

Psychedelics can inspire the "beginner's mind'.

One way to approach the question of relationship between psychedelics and meditation is to look at the meaning of the words independently. "Meditation" comes from the Latin "meditari", which is related to indo-Germanic "med", having something to do with "measuring, walking, staking out". We could define meditation as the act of exploring, walking in, measuring, staking out the sphere of consciousness. "Psychedelic" is based on the Greek words "psyche" and "delos", the first meaning "breath, the seat of consciousness", the second "clear, visible". Psychedelics can help to clear the mind to explore consciousness.

An Attitude

Beginner's mind is an attitude of openness, eagerness, and lack of preconceptions when studying a subject, even when studying at an advanced level, just as a beginner in that subject would. The term is especially used in the study of Zen Buddhism and Japanese martial arts.

The phrase is also used in the title of the book, Zen Mind, Beginner's Mind by the Zen teacher Shunryu Suzuki, who says the following about the correct approach to Zen practice: "*In the beginner's mind there are many possibilities, in the expert's mind there are few.*"

When using your beginner's mind you temporarily set all that you "know" aside, on purpose, for a while, and do as the teacher suggests—no matter how illogical, or insignificant, or meaningless it may seem to be—so that you can see what your experience is.

> *Beginner's mind is an attitude of openness, eagerness, and lack of preconceptions.*

There are many little exercises that don't seem to be important, or make sense when exploring experiential work. Opinions get in your way. None of these little exercises is going to permanently change you in any way. Yet each of them is designed to show you one more little integer of experience, one more facet of a whole experience of being awake and experiencing "the totality of the here and now."

Someone once said that "'I don't know" is the warrior's wisdom. When you hear yourself saying or thinking this--whatever you are doing at the time--it is a very good sign that insights and under-standings are going to be coming up. "I don't know" can give great relief of stress.

We always think we know. It is a tremendous burden. Most of the time when people think they know, they don't really know at all. All they know are their past impressions of the situation that is happening now, the conclusions they came to on previous times, or judgments about similar events or circumstances that happened once upon a time.

"I know" attitude is a tremendous handicap that keeps us living in the past. And out of touch with the present. It doesn't allow anything new, no surprises, no insights, no discoveries. It doesn't allow us to unlock the mysteries of the present moment, and it keeps us frozen in the judgments of the past.

The beginner's mind is a wonderful strategy to learn about the deeper mysteries of life. It isn't easy! There's nothing we treasure as much as our brilliant opinions and cherished beliefs. But they do not help us in finding new dimensions of life.

Beginner's mind doesn't ask you to believe in anything in particular. It simply says put aside the beliefs you already have for a little while, and do what the teacher suggests without beliefs or expectations, simply to see in your own direct experience whatever your experience is.

Whenever you want you can take back your opinions, reasoning and logic, your cherished beliefs--just the way you left them! Beginner's mind is simply recognizing your wonderful intellectual thinking mind that at times, distort things and block things off from our view. If we consciously set aside this effect, on purpose--for convention's sake, or for the fun of it will do--if we adopt "I don't know" as a strategy, instead, then secrets begin to become known.

Dangers of Psychedelics

Are there any dangers involved with the use of psychedelics? Yes, there are. They are very powerful sacraments, or medicine, and they have to be approached with the utmost respect, preferably under the guidance of an experienced friend. The fears most commonly voiced are damage to body and brain as well as dangerous behavior and addiction. The classic psychedelics, unlike substances such as heroin, cocaine, and alcohol, have virtually no organic toxicity in the quantities in which they are ingested. Their addictive risk is too small to be measured when used in ceremonial settings. Psychedelic traditions from the Vedic dawn to Eleusis to the Native American Church have succeeded in creating ritual contexts in which hazardous acting-out is virtually unknown.

Psychedelics can trigger dramatic changes in the psyche and spirit, the heart/mind, in consciousness. Of course this effect is the very reason for taking them in the first place. Is it ultimately helpful or harmful?

Buddha recommends to view our life "as a dream, a flash in the darkness, a star in the morning dawn, a bubble in a stream, an illusion of the senses". The aim of practice is to wake up from that dream. One question often asked after a deep experience is: Was it a genuine awakening, or was it just another dream within a dream, another illusion within an illusion?

A primary religious experience is the seed for a spiritual life. No matter how genuine the encounter with the Ultimate might be, it does not guarantee a genuine spiritual life. The experience may be authentic, but what counts is our daily life. Will we be able to muster up the necessary determination and patience to let the light that we glimpsed for a moment, be it through meditation or psychedelics, gradually penetrate our whole being? Will we allow the experience of oneness and belonging - whether or not it wasn't really real - to inspire and transform our lives? This is our challenge and our hope, individually and as a species.

27

MEDITATION

First, let us be aware of some of the ways in which this word "meditation" is used. It is sometimes used to mean a process of mental training, in which the attention is focused on a single idea or object. Second, some have used it to mean sitting for psychic development. Third, it is used by those on the spiritual Path, who are seeking for Self-realization, as applying to a technique for spiritual growth.

Meditation, as a technique for spiritual growth, has been practiced and recommended by all the great spiritual teachers and leaders, of all religions and cultures; but in our western world of today, the emphasis has swung to the opposite extreme of activity. "Service to others" is our motto - often, it seems, without regard to whether the service given was either directed by intelligence or motivated by love; or even desired by the recipient!

To restore balance to our spiritual growth, and hence the real value of our service to others, we need to learn and practice this ancient Way of Self-discovery; for in coming to know the Inner Being which is the real Self of each of us, we find true love for both God and neighbor, and our ability for real service is thereby increased. Can one whose well is dry give water to the thirsty ?

Wei Lang (China, 638-713) remarks that "What I can tell you is not Truth; but if you will turn the light of consciousness within yourself, there you will find Truth!" Truth is not in words, but in experience, of which words can be only a pale shadow. But even a shadow can be useful, if it directs our attention to the Reality which has produced it.

In directing our attention within, what do we find? Usually a jumble of thoughts and feelings; desires, frustrations, ambitions, fears, loves, hates, attractions, repulsions. If we can, even for a moment, command this storm, as a Teacher once did, "Peace! Be still!"- then, in the moment of calm, when all of these waves of thought and emotion have died down, we can see, find, experience, Truth. We can see, and become "The I Am", "The Self", "The Inner Light", "The Christ", which is One with The Father.

Or, if we can experience for a moment what we find within when someone unexpectedly calls, loudly, "LISTEN!", and we pause, alertly expectant, without thought or feeling, but just being open and perceptive, and receptive, we will find this same State of Being, which is not a "nothingness", nor a blankness, but a total Awareness, an Awakeness, which is Being Itself!

Or, if we will quietly and calmly observe within, watching the jumble of thoughts and feelings, we will find that the usual "inner storm" will slowly subside. Thoughts will become more widely spaced, do not follow each other quite so closely, until we wll be able to find a "space", an interval, between the thoughts. If we will then at once dive into this space, we will find ourselves within our own

Inner Being; we will have found the "Self, which is one with the Father - which, indeed, is the Father, for there is no separation. To find this is to fulfill the prayer of Jesus, "that they might be one as we are one"- that we might find the same oneness with the Father that he had found. Did He not say, "What I have done, you can do also!"?

When we build our 'house" on this Rock of Being, which is The Christ, instead of on the shifting sands of thought and emotion, we find the inner tranquillity which no storm in the external world can destroy; and we find ourselves becoming an increasingly clear channel through which Love can be expressed in Service.

A single experience of this Inner Light, or Self, can provide a stimulus to motivate us to further seeking. The path to this Center of our Being has been clearly marked by those who have gone before, but we ourselves must walk therein. In the beginning, at least, we need a daily regular time and place; perhaps a special corner, a special chair; when possible, a special room. For we are creatures of habit, and the development of helpful habits can save us time in the end. At first, as we seek this Mental Quiet, this inner peace and tranquillity, we catch only glimpses of the Inner Being; but gradually we acquire the ability to retain this awareness for a longer and longer time, until at last all of our living is irradiated by this glow from within. Then we have "removed our Light from underneath the bushel, and set it on the lamp-stand, so that it sheds light on all that is in the house" of our mind.

In the earlier stages of our following on the spiritual Path, we are likely to become discouraged if spectacular results are not achieved quickly. And yet we understand perfectly that time and endless effort are required if one is to achieve proficiency in any of the arts or sciences! Spiritual growth involves a lifetime of devotion and effort, and growth is usually unseen and un-noticed! On the spiritual Path, no effort made in sincerity is ever lost or wasted.

While at first we need to have a regular time and place, this inward turning for Mental Quiet can soon be practiced at any time, any place, under any circumstances. A voice student needs to have an hour daily devoted to the special practice of his exercises, but while this special time and place are necessary, he can also practice at any time, or in any place, whenever he chooses to do so. Ultimately, if he is a true musician, he no longer sings the music, but the music sings him!

When we have found, and become, this Inner Being, this Inward Light, how can we describe it? Words are such pale shadows! Perhaps it can be done only by saying what it is not! Has this Light any color ? or shape ? or size ? Is it related to time or space, to sound or silence?

Or do all of these originate from within this Inner Self? Is not this the finding of "The Christ, which is the Light of the World"? "The peace which passes understanding", the tranquillity which transcends that of the intellect ? Is not this true at-one-ment with the Father ? "You ARE the Light of the world" and for one who IS the Light, there are no shadows!

May you then find this deep Center of Being, this Indwelling Christ, the Inward Light, the Atman, Nirvana, The Void for which all names and descriptions are meaningless ! If you will seek, with your whole heart, you shall find!

28

DEALING WITH THE SHADOW

As Jung indicated, the Shadow holds all the material that we have pushed aside so we can hide from ourselves. Unfortunately, it also contains much of our energy, and as long as it is unconscious, it exerts a powerful influence on our behavior without our knowing it. Furthermore, Shadow material is responsible for most of the difficulties humans create in the world. We project our Shadow onto others, believe those others to be the source of our difficulties, and seek refuge from them rather than taking responsibility in our own hands. Consequently we must resolve Shadow material if we are to develop. If this were accomplished on a widespread basis, it would be a major benefit for the world.

Jung describes human development as the process of "making the unconscious conscious." Psychedelics, particularly in low doses, can be an extremely effective tool in this process. The bulk of my experience is with the phenethylamine compounds, which remained legal longer than the standard psychedelics such as LSD, mescaline, and psilocybin. Whereas a full dose of a phenethylamine like 2C-T-2 or 2C-T-7 might be 20 milligrams, a low dose would be ten or twelve milligrams, or roughly equivalent to 25-50 micrograms of LSD.

The most infallible guide to Shadow material is our uncomfortable feelings. Many do not like to use low doses because these feelings come to the surface. Rather than experience them, they use larger doses to transcend them. But these uncomfortable feelings are precisely what we must resolve to free ourselves from the Shadow, gain strength and energy, and function more comfortably and competently in the world. By using smaller amounts and being willing to focus our full attention on whatever feelings arise and breathe through them, we find that these feelings eventually dissolve, often with fresh insight and understanding of our personal dynamics. The release of such material permits an expansion of awareness and energy. If we work persistently to clear away repressed areas, we can enter the same sublime states that are available with larger doses—with an important additional gain. Having resolved our uncomfortable feelings, we are in a much better position to maintain a high state of clarity and functioning in day-to-day life.

I would also like to add a word about frequency: Individuals vary greatly in their frequency of use of these materials. Some are satisfied with an overwhelming experience which they feel is good for a lifetime. Others wish to renew their acquaintance with these areas once or twice a year. Still others are interested in frequent explorations to continually push their knowledge forward. Regardless of the frequency, it is wise to make sure that the previous experience has been well integrated before embarking on the next one. Early in one's contact with these substances, where there is a wealth of new experience, this may take several months. As one becomes more experienced, the integration time grows shorter, and the interval between trials may be shortened.

Many stop the use of psychedelics when they feel they have learned what they wished. But often it is likely that they halt because they have hit a deeply repressed, painful area that is heavily defended. The issue goes beyond purely personal material, however. One is unlikely to reach full realization without awareness, not merely of one's own pain and suffering, but of that of all mankind. This may help explain the Dark Night of the Soul, which is the final barrier to mystical union described by Evelyn Underhill in her classic book Mysticism.Since we are one, we must not only confront the personal Shadow, but the Shadow of all humanity. We can do this more readily when we discover the ample love that is available to dissolve all Shadow material.

HOMAGE TO
THE AWE-FULL SEER

At each beat
in the Earth's rotating dance
there is born "   "
a momentary cluster of molecules
possessing the tranient ability to know-see-experience
its own place in the evolutionary spiral.

Such an organism, such an event
senses exactly where he or she is
in the billion-year-old ballet.

Thay are able to trace back
the history of the deoxyribonucleic thread
of which they are both conductive element and current.
They can experience the next moment
in its million to the millionth meaning.
Exactly that.

Some divine seers are recognized for this unique capacity.
Those that are recognized
are called and killed by various names.
Most of them are not recognized—
they float through life
like a snowflake
kissing the earth.

No one ever hears them murmur "Ah there"
At the moment of impact.
Seers are aware of each other's existence
the way each particle in the hurtling nuclear trapeze
is aware of other particles.
They move too fast to give names
to themselves or each other.

Such people can be described in terms
no more precise or less foolish
than the descriptive equations of nuclear physics.
They have no more or less meaning
in the cultural games of life
than electrons have in the game of chess.
They are present but cannot be perceived or categorized.
They exist at a level beyond
the black and white squares of the game board. The
function of "   " is to teach.

Take an apple and slice it down the middle.
A thin red circle surrounds the gleaming white meat.
In the center is a dark seed
whose function is beyond any of your games.
If you knew how to listen
the seed would hum you a seed-song.

The divine incarnates teach
like a snowflake caught in the hand teaches.
Once you speak the message you have lost it.
Once you know the message you no longer have it.
The seed becomes a dried pit, the snowflake
a film of water on your hand.

Wise seers are continually
exploding in beautiful dance.
Like a speckled fish
dying in your hand
as its eye look at you unblinking.
Like the virus fragmenting
divine beauty in the grasp of tissue.

Now and then the "   " sings
words beyond rational comprehension.
The message is always the same
though the sounds, the scratched rhumba
of inkmarks is always different.

It's like Einstein's equation felt as orgasm.
The serpent unwinds up the spine,
mushrooms like a lotus sunflare in the skull.
If I tell you that the apple seed message hums the drone
of a hindu flute
will that stop the drone?

The secret of "   " must always be secret.
Divine sage recognized, message lost.
Snowflake caught, pattern changed.
They dance our the pattern without being recognized.
Caught in the act, they melt in your hand.

The message then contained in a drop of water
involves another chase for the infinite.
The sign of "   " is change and anonymity.
As soon as you try to glorify
sanctify, worship, deify the seer
you have killed him.

Thus the Pharisees
performed a merry, holy ballet.
All praise to them!
It is the Christians who kill Christ.
As soon as you invent a symbol
give "   " a name
you assassinate the process
to serve your own ends.

To speak the name of Buddha
Christ or Lao Tse—
except as a sudden ecstatic breath—
is to murder the living God
fix him with your preservative
razor him onto a microscope slide
sell him for profit in your biological supply house.

The seers have no function
but they produce in others the ecstatic gasp
the uncontrollable visionary laugh.
Too much!
So What!
Why not!
The stark stare of wonder
Awful!

Awe-full!

From *Psychedelic Prayers & Other Meditations*, Timothy Leary, Ronin, 1997.

by permission

About the Author

Although John Aiken and his wife Louise have an important place in the psychedelic chronicles, their story is poorly documented. They were MD's by profession and in the later years of their lives they retired to New Mexico for spiritual research, with and without psychedelics. Art Kleps has credited their Church Of Awakening as being the very first non-Native American psychedelic church to be registered (1963), predating both Kleps and the Millbrooks by a couple of years.

Drawing on a vast array of ancient and modern sources, Aiken presents an esoteric doctrine of self-realization and ultimate transcendence, told in a pure, stripped-down style that displays self-confidence and insight. It is not a rehash but a new psychedelic path, with vedic-yogic as well as Christian and Native American influences. The book contains a couple of trip reports, including one from an Indian guru, who does a respectworthy attempt to squeeze the cosmologic-metaphysic experiences of an acid trip into plain English. Written mainly in 1963, Aiken's LSD vibe is very different from what would follow, and deserves much greater recognition.

RONIN

Books for Independent Minds

Visit Ronin Publishing

at www.roninpub

and enjoy!

Use isbn to order from any bookstore,
Amazon and other online outlets.

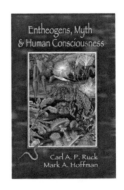

Bookstores: Order from PGW

CPSIA information can be obtained
at www.ICGtesting.com
Printed in the USA
LVOW11s1041141216
517216LV00006B/51/P

9 781579 512323